GROTTON REVISITED

... Planning in Crisis?

GROTTON REVISITED

... Planning in Crisis?

An illustrated handbook for delegates to the Planning in Crisis conference to be held at the ~~Polytechnic~~ University (pending) of Central Grotton, 5–9 September 2010

Steve Ankers, David Kaiserman and Chris Shepley

Routledge
Taylor & Francis Group

LONDON AND NEW YORK

This book is dedicated to Margaret Ankers, Veronica Kaiserman and Jan Shepley, who have had to put up with quite a lot.

This edition published 2010
by Routledge
2 Park Square, Milton Park, Abingdon, Oxon, OX14 4RN

Simultaneously published in the USA and Canada
by Routledge
270 Madison Avenue, New York, NY 10016

Routledge is an imprint of the Taylor & Francis Group, an informa business

Designed and typeset by Alex Lazarou
Printed and bound by Grafos SA, Barcelona, Spain

British Library Cataloguing in Publication Data
A catalogue record for this book is available from the British Library

Library of Congress Cataloging-in-Publication Data
Ankers, Stephen.
Grotton revisited : planning in crisis? / Steve Ankers, David Kaiserman, Chris Shepley.
    p. cm.
Includes bibliographical references and index.
1. City planning—Great Britain—Humor. 2. Regional planning—Great Britain—Humor.
I. Kaiserman, David. II. Shepley, Chris. III. Title.
HT169.G7A68 2010
307.1'216209427393—dc22

                                                                    2009046602

ISBN10: 0-415-54646-X (hbk)
ISBN10: 0-415-54647-8 (pbk)
ISBN13: 978-0-415-54646-1 (hbk)
ISBN13: 978-0-415-54647-8 (pbk)

Images credits:
For the image of the caravan tower block (from an open-air play by Tsjechov in the
Amsterdamse Bos) – © Henk Jan Bouwmeester, Amsterdam
For the image of Scrabble – SCRABBLE® is a registered trademark of J.W. Spear and
Sons, Ltd, Maidenhead SL6 4UB, England, under licence from Mattel Europa BV, a
subsidiary of Mattel Inc, © Mattel 2009. All rights reserved.
SCRABBLE, the distinctive game board and letter tiles, and all associated logos are
trademarks of Hasbro in the United States and Canada and are used with permission.
© 2009 Hasbro. All rights reserved.
For the image of the gnome on the cover © Jozsef Szasz-Fabian I Dreamstime.com

Contents

Biographies

STEVE ANKERS was Assistant Director responsible for environment, countryside management, economic development, transport planning and road safety at East Sussex County Council. He was previously Head of Countryside Planning at Greater Manchester Council and then Director of Greater Manchester Countryside Unit. He has served on various national bodies including the UK Biodiversity Steering Group, National Coasts and Estuaries Advisory Group, Countryside Recreation Research Advisory Group, Countryside Staff Training Advisory Group, and was Advisor to the Association of Metropolitan Authorities (AMA) on Countryside and Wildlife. He now works part-time as Planning Officer for the South Downs Society, while worrying about his global footprint and Liverpool FC.

DAVID KAISERMAN worked as a town planner for 30 years with Manchester City Council and the Greater Manchester Council. During this time, he led teams which prepared the county's green belt and the City Council's first Unitary Development Plan, and played a major role in a number of high-profile public inquiries. In 1996 he left the post of Acting Director of Planning and Environmental Health at the City and joined TRA Ltd as a Senior Associate, providing training and consultancy support for local authority planners and elected members. At the same time he became a Consultant Planning Inspector. Since 2007 he has been trying to avoid having anything to do with writing this book.

CHRIS SHEPLEY CBE was the Chief Planning Inspector from 1994 to 2002. Previously he was Director of Development at Plymouth City Council (1985–1994), and held various posts including Deputy County Planning Officer at Greater Manchester Council (1973–1985), and at Manchester City Council (1966–1973). He was President of the RTPI in 1989. He is Honorary Visiting Professor at the University of Westminster and held a similar post at the University of Manchester (1990–1994). He has an Honorary DSc from the University of the West of England. He is on the RTPI General Assembly, and the Policy Council of the Town and Country Planning Association (TCPA), has been on the Council of the European Council of Town Planners and the Planning Aid Council, and is a trustee of the Theatres Trust. He writes a regular column in 'Planning'. He now works as an independent planning consultant. He also grumbles competently.

Acknowledgements

The authors wish to thank: Dave Charlesworth for bringing to life the Pig's Ear scheme so convincingly; Dave Smith for his vision of Muckthorpe Bottoms; Dave Evans for the gnomes; Alan Wenban-Smith for the technical realisation of the business plan layout; 4NW – the Regional Leaders Board, for the plan on the cover; Jan Molyneux for the questionnaire; Jo Nightingale for Dunromin's helpful web page; and Simon Walmsley for making the Decide-o-Matic. They are also indebted to Paul Barnard and Jonathan Bell of Plymouth City Council, Simon Hickmott and John Robbins of East Sussex County Council, Andy and others at GL Hearn (Bath), and all those other friends and colleagues who helped by making suggestions, reading text, pretending to laugh in the right places, and in many other ways. They are particularly grateful to Robert Upton, who got the ball rolling, Alex Lazarou for his design skills, and to all the people at the RTPI and Routledge who have made it happen.

The President of the Royal Town Planning Institute (RTPI)

What an honour and a privilege it is to be asked to declare this handbook open – truly the pinnacle of a challenging Presidential year. There is no doubt in my mind, such as it is, that the great Conference of 2010 will go down as a watermark in the development of town and country planning in Britain. I am particularly delighted that Grotton, of all places, will be acting as the host to this magnificent occasion which will, coincidentally, mark the 259th anniversary of Capability Brown's famous visit to the town in 1751. I am sure Capability, had he been alive today, would have been the first to agree with me.

I am determined that my Presidential initiative in not preventing the publication of this book shall be a resounding success – and I do mean *success* – we should not be ashamed of saying so. I sometimes think that 'success' today has become something of a dirty word, like 'botty' or 'barn conversion'. Yet I well remember as a young planner I once met Sir Patrick Abercrombie. I shall never forget his words to me: 'Go and get on with your work' he said, in that deep, friendly voice of his. What good advice that was.

I want to thank everyone involved at Grotton County Council for organising the conference. There is a lot of work in arranging these things, I am told, and in a hard pressed department it can be the last straw which sinks the camel completely.

But now the ball is on the other foot, the preliminaries are over, and the real business starts. There may be troubles ahead. Sometimes we may be treading on thin water. But I can safely say that, when you look back after the conference, your few short days in Grotton will have put your own problems into perspective. As Beaujolais rightly said, '*Il y a toujours quelqu'un plus mal que vous-même*'.

When all is said and done, and when one considers the age in which we live, with its declining standards, increasing violence, spatial planning, and incessant rain, and were it not for the open-ended commitment to broadening ideological synchronicity within and beyond the profession and the increasing climate thingy and social and economic attitudes leading inexorably to what can only be described as a state of transition.

But things are not always so clear-cut, as the wonderful speakers at the conference will be quick to elucify. I am only sorry that owing to prior commitments I will not be able to be there myself.

Encomium by

The Very Rev Amos Tite
Bishop of all the Grottons

In responding to the kind invitation by the organisers of this grand convocation to say a few words – and I really do mean a *few* – I can do no better than to read to you a short extract from the Book of Regulations, verses 22 to 24:

22.   And Ezekiel dwelt in the land of the Hittites. And he came unto the city of Gonad, which is in Ephesus, just north of Psoriasis, and did dwell there for three days and three nights, and did feast greatly at the table of the high priests.

23.   And on the fourth night there came an great wind. And Ezekiel fell down upon his knees and smote the ground, saying, Lord, why hast thou visited this affliction upon me? And the Lord answered, saying, knowest thou nought? For it is written, he that shall feast greatly upon the fruits of the earth shall be visited by an great wind.

24.   And it came to pass that the wind did rise up against the temple of Gonad, and its walls did crack with an great roar, and did fall down upon the heads of all the people and they perished, mostly. The end.

We can, I think, draw two principal lessons from Ezekiel's painful experience, lessons which, it is surely not too fanciful to suggest, are both startlingly contemporary, yet astonishingly ageless in their message; clear and absolutely unequivocal in their meaning, while managing to remain, at the same time, wholly unfathomable.

Most of you taking part in this great gathering will not need me to point out the continuing significance and relevance of these words. The parable of the Great Wind and the Temple speaks to us, does it not, of the wisdom of thinking ahead – of, in short, *planning*. Even during his time of exile, when you would have thought he would have had other things to worry about, Ezekiel appears acutely conscious of Man's folly in ignoring the perils of climate change, and even of the need to ensure that the requirements of the Building Regulations are always fully complied with.

His warnings continue to sound down the ages. I am often reminded[1]

---

1 Publisher's note: we are not at all sure why the Rev Tite's encomium ends here, but have decided it would be a kindness not to trouble him further on the matter.

GROTTON REVISITED

... Planning in Crisis?

The precise location of Grotton has puzzled geographers throughout the ages

chapter one

Planning in Crisis

Some Aspects of the Great Conference of 1979 and Cautious Conclusions on its Impact on the Development and Growth of Grotton and on the Evolution of Planning and Related Studies to 2010 or so

By Deirdre Sulkie
Routledge Professor of Historical and Environmental Semantics, ~~Polytechnic~~ University (pending) of Central Grotton

NOTE: we are particularly grateful to Prof Sulkie for this survey of the recent history of planning in Grotton, which, at the request of the authors, she kindly contributed to this volume, shortly before she began legal proceedings against the ~~Polytechnic~~ University (pending). We wish her well in her retirement.

In 2007, Prof Sulkie received a bronze medal in the ESRC's annual award for the Most Optimistically Worded Grant Application.[1]

1979 was a millstone in the history of town and country planning. There will be few who, like me, had the privilege of being in Grotton during that vestigial year, and who will fail to remember – or at least be unable to forget – the significance, the excitement, the paracetamol and what was memorably termed by myself as the *Belanglosigkeit* of it all. It is partly for their benefit that the authors of this important book have come to me for a brief account of that remarkable period and its impact on Western European thought.

Of course, anyone who is anyone in this field will have read *The Grotton Papers*[2] – generally regarded in academic circles as the most significant critique of the planning process ever written (with the possible exception of my own *Mediation of Space – Making of Place: Speculations on the meaning of the Royal Town Planning Institute's logo*[3]). *The Grotton Papers* served as background reading for the thousands of delegates who flocked to the city in September of that heady year, to attend 'Planning in Crisis', the now almost-forgotten conference which, it is no exaggeration to state, altered the way people thought about Ashton-under-Lyne.

'Planning in Crisis' could, of course, have been the title of any conference held in Britain on this most misunderstood of subjects since at least the fourteenth century. But my researches suggest that this one was different. It turned out, as those who were fortunate enough to be there will attest, to be seminal. Not just because of the salmonella in the Digites de Poisson served at the Conference Dinner, which sent so many speeding home with a following wind; nor because of the unforgettable spectacle of the shimmering cascade of water sparkling in the sun as it rippled and babbled effulgently down the Town Hall steps following a leak in the Members' lavatory. Without doubt, what made Grotton '79 so significant was the quality of the papers which were presented – all of them influential, innovative, formative, ground-breaking, pioneering, original and earth-shattering.[4]

---

1 As all really important academics know, the ESRC, formerly the SSRC of course, facilitates applications to the RAE which then enables HEIs to apply to HEFCE for funding based on the 67 UOAs, with guidance from the HESA (who represent UUK and GHE, which took the place of SCOP).

2 *The Grotton Papers*, Ankers, Kaiserman and Shepley, RTPI 1979, pp 78, out of print, slightly foxed.

3 Sulkie D. In: *Zeitschrift für die Hoffnungslosesten Planungsabteilung*, vol xxxiii. Darmstadt, pp 12–233.

4 *Roget's Thesaurus* 1972.

How fortunate, therefore, that at the very moment that Grotton County Council has achieved 'Average and with Moderate Prospects of Remaining Average' in the annual Comprehensive Area Assessment, the full, unexpurgated record of the proceedings of that first iconic event should have been released by the Government under the thirty-year rule.

The Most Exciting Thing for Me

And the most exciting thing for me is that exactly ~~thirty~~ thirty-one years after that great gathering, I find myself making yet another major contribution to a conference entitled 'Planning in Crisis'. Three questions immediately arise. What lessons are to be learned? Why now? Why Grotton? And how much will I be paid? This remarkable book is designed to provide some of the answers – and will, I am sure, point up the need for further research in the very areas where my own modest expertise allows me to be of particular value.

My task is quite simply to summarise the history of modern planning, with particular reference to the 1979 Conference, in no more than 1000 unplagiarised words (I will obviously exceed that, being an academic). So that is what I will do.

The 1979 Predicament

The former Greater Grotton Metropolitan County Council, now almost forgotten, was created by mistake. The old Ministry of Housing and Local Government had special skill in this direction, which has of course been developed, refined and hugely extended by its successor departments. But this particular error was of more than usual significance, for it led (albeit unintentionally) to a golden age of metropolitan planning, thanks largely to the efforts of its charismatic Chief Planning Officer, T Break. The County, together with (or, more usually, despite) its district counterparts in the City of Grotton, Dunromin, Golden Delicious, Grimethwaite and Cloggley, developed new approaches to planning, the like of which had never been seen before and may well never be seen again.

It is important for the reader to understand the nature of these District Councils. I have delegated this task to the Assistant Tutor in Perfunctory Geographical Antithetics, who is always appreciative of the opportunity to fill in the detail for me when

I run out of time. His or her meanderings will, I imagine, be useful in concocting subsequent chapters.

When I was at school, Applied Grotton Studies was an essential part of the curriculum, unlike the modern obsession with such things as reading, speling and the like. Older readers will remember the first time they realised the significance of the fact that Grotton lies roughly half way between Venus and Mars, at a crossing point of the River Grime:

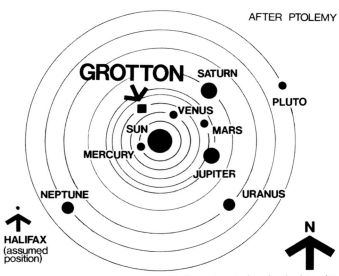

Consequently, as a communications hub it knows no equals, having few communications with anywhere worth speaking of. But its position almost exactly equidistant between London, Dublin, Edinburgh and a point in the North Sea fifty miles east of Grimsby has for years given it a unique advantage over other conurbations of a similar size.

The Pennines, which have long provided a cultural and economic barrier between Yorkshire and the civilised world, bound the county to the east; this causes the prevailing westerly winds to rise and via a process of catalytic conversion to drop their moisture on the Grotton Plain accounting, it is widely believed, for the morose disposition of many of the inhabitants.

Planning through the Ages

What then were the causes of the crisis which befell the County in the late 1970s? The available research suggests that there were three, which I will call (a), (b) and (c).[5] But in addition, understanding the history of planning in Grotton is vitally important if the reader is to appreciate the current problems of the town and its sub-region.

The Domesday Report of Survey carried out in 1086 by W Conqueror and Partners records that, at that time, Grotton comprised three feoff-gelds, eight scutages and a pig – giving an indication of its importance in the economic and cultural life of the region. Although in some need of revision, this Survey is still used for the purposes of development control.

Unsurprisingly, during the years that have elapsed since, Grotton has faced numerous planning challenges and has, at times of particular change and stress, responded through the well-tried means of bringing together the greatest minds of the day, to see if they could come up with anything useful.

As early as the fourteenth century, for example, Grotton's Planning in Crisis Conference addressed the Government's failure in 1350 to foresee the impact of the Black Death on national population and household forecasts. These had delayed the preparation of the Corre Strattegie for the Hundred of Bletherley to such an extent that it was completely out of date before Baron T Breque was able to present it to public inquiry.

The Planning in Crisis Conference in 1539 followed the Dissolution of Slattocks Monastery. Recent excavations in the Waitrose car park provide compelling evidence that the monks, led by Father T Break, had been distilling a cross between mead and lighter fuel for sale at local witch-burnings, which even in those days constituted a material change of use, since they took place on more than twenty-eight days a year. (It is interesting to note that the local magistrates only fined them fifteen groats and a case of Benedictine, prompting a complaint from local residents, bearing placards outside the conference, that enforcement was not being taken seriously by the authorities.)

The Conference of 1667 considered the planning implications of the Great Fire of Grotton, which has been largely ignored by scholars, who have always been more interested in the headline-grabbing blaze in London a year earlier. The inspiring story of that disaster, still retold each year on its anniversary, when the town's schoolchildren take to the streets gaily setting fire to anyone thought to be from Liverpool, turns out to be apocryphal. The mayor of Grotton at that time, Sir T Break the First (or the Sixth of Scotland), did not, as was once thought, attempt to smother the flames with the only copy of the emerging Grotton Structure Plan,[6] for the simple reason that he was at the theatre, pretending to laugh at jokes in *Chlamydia: or The Coxcomb Reveng'd* by Beaumont and Fletcher.

Break did, however, play a leading role in the astonishing revival of the town, albeit with considerable help from Sir Christopher Wren's brother Frank Lloyd Wren, whose mother-in-law came from Muckthorpe. Wren's proposal that the Methodist Chapel should be replaced with a shard of glass was controversial from the start, especially since no one at that time had heard of Methodism. What is more, letters to the local paper (which could not unfortunately be published until 1888 when the *Grotton Advertiser* was launched) demanded that new buildings were designed to match the old (which consisted mainly of characterfully charred and deformed timbers).

But Wren stood his ground. He argued that a Gherkin and a 1930s wireless were just the ticket if regeneration was required, though he had no idea what a 1930s wireless looked like, or indeed what a wireless was, or indeed a wire. In what was to become the world's first Design and Access Statement he declared: '*Respect for the genius loci demands a demonstrably post-modernist appraisal of the inherent urbanity of the locale, the palpability of the position, the setting of the situation, which implies an architectural response which is grand yet modest, imposing yet intimate, huge yet tiny; one which clearly implies that the architect in question has reproductive equipment of the most enormous size, without suggesting to a sceptical public that he is merely compensating for inadequacies in this department; one which will place Grotton on the world map and attract a load of compleat bankers to the town; one which my practice is ideally placed to undertake*'.

After that things began to gather pace. The 1720 Planning in Crisis Conference considered the South Sea Bubble and its impact on the housing market. Lord T Break of Upton-on-t'Bogg, himself suffering from both negative equity and quantitative easing, chaired a session on social housing. The 1793 Conference was held primarily to consider the impact of the French Revolution on British planning thought. The Reign of Terror had put the wind up the planning department, and proposals to limit the amount of sedan chair parking in the town centre had to be postponed.

5 Sulkie D (Ed). *New Mexico Journal of Probability and Stochastic Processes, Vol 1 1999* (there is no Vol 2).

6 Prepared in 1631 and approved by the Secretary of State in 1974.

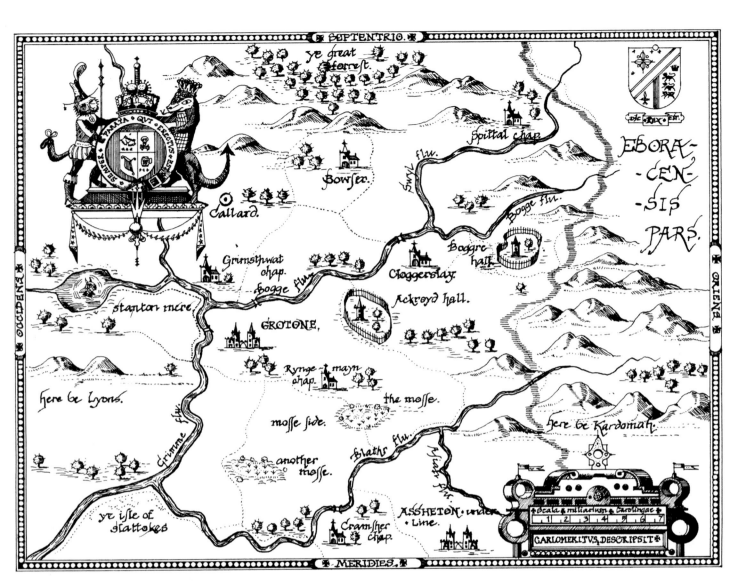

Grotton in the late seventeenth century

Grotton colliery magnate Theophilus Break was arguably the most influential Victorian of his day. Industrialist, philanthropist and bigamist, he scoured the Empire to create the finest collection of useless artefacts ever assembled in one place. The result was the Really Great Exhibition of 1850. The Planning in Crisis Conference held in the ground-breaking new exhibition hall was unfortunately interrupted during the Minister's launch of a new Planning Policy Statement on high speed rail services, when fire broke out. In a similar incident the following year, the Crystal Palace took some five hours to burn down: sadly, the

Great Hall of Grotton, being made entirely from coal, took just twenty minutes.

The Planning in Crisis Conference of 1919 was held in the shadow of war. The profession's response to the conflagration was to advocate a new town, and Ebenezer Howard turned the first sod at the Sleightley Garden Suburb during the conference. However, the wartime carnage had played havoc with the population forecasts, and the development was never completed, or indeed, started (although lawyers have recently concluded that turning the first sod did constitute the commencement of development within the meaning of the Act).

Smarting from the loss of the 1936 Olympic Games to Berlin, Grotton compensated by holding the 1936 Planning in Crisis Conference to discuss the previous year's Restriction of Ribbon Development Act, and how Grotton could accommodate the need for all those ribbons. T Break's invitation to von Ribbontrop to address the delegates was frustrated by visa problems; his apparent intention to advocate the annexation of Dukinfield clearly counted against him.

1947 saw the great post-war renewal conference. Delegates were inspired by the words of Grotton's head of the planning service, General Commanding (Rationing, Procurement, Local Plans and Development Control) Tedder Break, and thrilled to discover that their profession was about to be invented. The 1947 Act, the 1949 National Parks and Access to the Countryside Act, and the rest were a natural culmination. Surveying the still-smouldering ruins of Grotton, Break reflected that it would be a long time before cheap jokes would be made about how the planners had done more damage to the town than the Luftwaffe.

Crowds line the route as the Queen arrives in Grotton for the Silver Jubilee celebrations

And so to 1979

And so to the Planning in Crisis Conference of 1979. As we have seen, Grotton had many times fallen into disrepair, dismay, disassemblage, dislocation, disaffection, disaster, disruption, dissipation, dishonour, disparagement, and disinfectant. Each time it had recovered through a combination of alliteration and hard work.

By 1979 the area had fallen on hard times once again. The 1970s had been a difficult period for proud northern metropolises (metropolice?). Though some had enjoyed the three day week, student planners in particular found that working for three days was quite a challenge, and morale in the six planning departments was generally low.

What was worse was the fact that, for reasons we still cannot understand, the planners were operating in a complete vacuum. It seems scarcely credible that it had not dawned on civil servants that what local planning authorities had been doing up to that point had been immune from external scrutiny – *targets* in other words had not been invented.

Original research that I have undertaken into recently published research commissioned by Government (following preliminary scoping by a number of consultants, including myself)[7] shows conclusively that, during this period, planners had no idea what they were doing. Yes, they were making plans, deciding applications, reclaiming derelict land, mapping out a brighter future for the county and so on and so forth – but why? Who were the stakeholders? Where was the front-loading? Where, in short, was the empirical architecture which was capable of demonstrating, should it prove necessary, that local government was incompetent?

The unrelieved monotony of this – the soulless routine of actually doing planning, the wearisome stodginess of believing it was worthwhile – has thankfully now been removed, replaced by a simple need to meet a few elementary targets. Modern planners will find it almost impossible to understand how their predecessors survived with so few statistics to submit.

At some point, County Planning Officer T Break decided that running a major international conference would be a good way not only to help his team through this difficult period but to put Grotton back on the map where it belonged (rather than, say, in Peru), and invited his colleagues in the Districts

7 Sulkie D. *Spatial Dispersion of Interconnection Clusters within a Fuzzy Environment: a case study from Grimethwaite.* Subm to Regional Studies Assoc 1981, 1988, 1992. Unpubl. and unreadable to be honest.

to join him. Clearly conferences had been a successful tactic throughout Grotton's history, leading in every case to a period of resuscitation (or at least a period of stagnation, which in Grotton's case must be counted as a success). So that's what he did.

What Happened at the Conference?

You will want to know what happened at the conference.

Despite the arrival of the new Government, about which I have more to say below, the 1979 conference had a guardedly upbeat flavour, as the programme for the week clearly demonstrates.

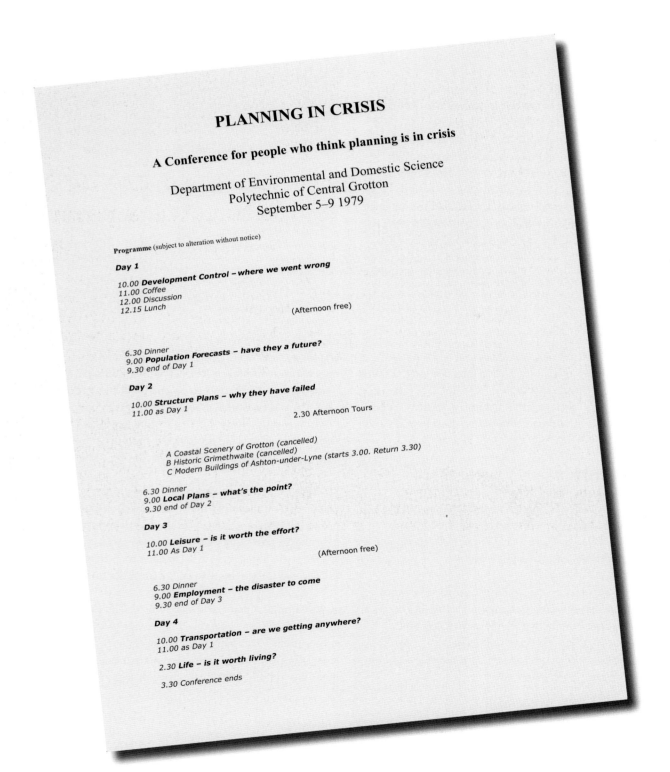

PLANNING IN CRISIS

A Conference for people who think planning is in crisis

Department of Environmental and Domestic Science
Polytechnic of Central Grotton
September 5–9 1979

Programme (subject to alteration without notice)

Day 1

10.00 **Development Control – where we went wrong**
11.00 Coffee
12.00 Discussion
12.15 Lunch

(Afternoon free)

6.30 Dinner
9.00 **Population Forecasts – have they a future?**
9.30 end of Day 1

Day 2

10.00 **Structure Plans – why they have failed**
11.00 as Day 1

2.30 Afternoon Tours

A Coastal Scenery of Grotton (cancelled)
B Historic Grimethwaite (cancelled)
C Modern Buildings of Ashton-under-Lyne (starts 3.00. Return 3.30)

6.30 Dinner
9.00 **Local Plans – what's the point?**
9.30 end of Day 2

Day 3

10.00 **Leisure – is it worth the effort?**
11.00 As Day 1

(Afternoon free)

6.30 Dinner
9.00 **Employment – the disaster to come**
9.30 end of Day 3

Day 4

10.00 **Transportation – are we getting anywhere?**
11.00 as Day 1

2.30 **Life – is it worth living?**

3.30 Conference ends

The conference attracted all the great thinkers of the day,[8] including myself, and left a lasting impression on all those who had the privilege of attending. 'This was a very remarkable event,' Sir Colin Buchanan was heard to exclaim; 'I have never experienced anything quite like that,' said Sir Desmond Heap; 'Happily I could not have anticipated such an occurrence,' said Ebenezer Howard (dec'd). 'What was all that about?' said Master J Gummer (16).

The *Grotton Advertiser* reported the event in its usual way:

Never having been ... life, complete shock to ... gusting offence, however clever.

Didn't deny that he would be ab... benefits, but sometimes liked to sunbathe naked. The Committee decided to have a site visit.

...epted that it was ... sonable and would make sure the stop-cock was open.

Planners Romp Ends in Wildlife Carnage

Grotton, Tuesday

There was outrage in Pussycat Mews this morning when a pigeon ate a sweet wrapper dropped by a delegate at the "Planning in Crisis" conference, and choked to death. Neighbour Miss Primrose Cottage said "I'm outraged. I have been feeding Chirpy the pigeon for several years. He was my angel". He is to be buried with full ornithological honours at the Dunromin Civic Amenity Site tomorrow.

T Break, the conference organiser, apologised. He said "I apologise. We are all very upset about the death of Chirpy, who was a much loved figure in the community and our first thoughts at this time are with the Columbidae family. I hope in due course they will be able to move on".

Det. Chief Supt. Gary Nackers said: "this is a decent young pigeon, and he's cut down in his prime while going about his lawful pecking on the public highway".

The Conference, which attracted delegates from all over parts of Europe, was about planning, or something.

Associated Press

Bishop denie... his wife's pan...

by James Grubb

Yesterday's disclosures followin... rowdy scenes in court were the wo... (66) said it was the first time he h... Magistrates heard that the bishop... only pretending", but that did n... wearing only a plastic cassock ... even on the bus, but he accepte... viously good character, despite... fined £6 with cos...

8 This unfortunately did not include the Secretary of State, a self-styled Mr Heseltine, who was busy locking jobs in a filing cabinet.

What did we Learn at the Conference?

You will want to know what were the key achievements of the conference. My research[9] shows quite clearly that there were three – let us call them (a), (b) and (f) – and they were to herald a turning point in the way academics like me assess the key lessons and findings from things like conferences. It is convenient to summarise them thus:

1. temporary permission should on no account be given for demolitions
2. if intending to travel to a conference by train, always check that the destination is connected to the rail network
3. Bletherley is twinned with the Dordogne town of L'Oréal – and they're not worth it

By any reckoning, these were considerable achievements. It is clear from interviews I have carried out with surviving delegates that several left the conference with a spring in their step, a song in their heart and a variety of sexually transmitted diseases. Hundreds of them were seen to run back to their desks, roll up their sleeves and finally water the spider plant, even before filling in their expenses claims. A new planning dawn had, well, dawned.

But there was a cloud in the woodpile.

Towards the Abyss

It will be recalled that the conference was held in September 1979. What was not predictable at the time was the full impact of the arrival that May of the Conservative Government led by the redoubtable Mrs Thatcher, apparently known as the Iron Maiden, or some other mediaeval means of torture.

Mrs Thatcher's success in dealing with the problems of mass employment in the Grotton area have been chronicled elsewhere,[10] but there can be little doubt that she was fully conscious of the importance of her programme (I personally was in Muckthorpe in 1982 when she was seen picking her way uncertainly across the windswept site of a former carbolic soap works, wiping tears from her eyes as she contemplated the stark reality of the human misery behind the latest factory closures. Either that or she had a cold).

It is tempting to conclude from the record of the times that the Conservative Government was (in the words of Arthur Scargill[11]) 'a psychotic bunch of free-market gangsters whose sole objective in life was to beat the workers into a whimpering pulp of castrated zombies'. But in my estimation, this assessment pays insufficient regard to the systemic weaknesses of Grotton's economic base.

It is generally forgotten, for example, that while shipbuilding was an early casualty of the Government's new strategy, this was largely because the town is not, and never has been, on the coast. The Blether Navigation had been widened in the 1890s, but usage was limited and it had gradually silted up. Only one sizeable vessel had been built since the war – the 'Alderman Grimshaw' – a coastal steamer named after the former Leader of the County Council. She is a glorious sight, a tribute to the shipbuilder's art, and can still be seen at the yard, being (like the Alderman himself) too broad to pass down the canal to the sea.

The Government moved on to close down sheep shearing (once a major industry in Cloggley), treacle making, and the manufacture of triangular nameplates for standing on end at Examinations in Public. Only Bletherley, the home of bankers, flankers and spankers, prospered, being full of rich people in nice clean jobs in financial services which earned wealth for Britain, and didn't have the potential to bring the country to its knees.

What was the policy response to this devastating collapse? Normally of course there would have been three of these; in this case however there were only two. The first was to pour millions of pounds into reducing bus fares and re-forming pit waste to make perfectly decent council housing; the second was to negotiate twinning arrangements with the Provisional IRA. Naturally, all this was anathema (I think that's the right word) to Mrs Thatcher, who predictably responded by seeking to abolish local government.

At the same time, her ministers came up with a whole series of initiatives designed to give planners one last chance to show why they should not all be stood up against a wall and shot. They felt that planning might be getting in the way of people being allowed to do whatever they wanted, wherever they wanted. (The Royal Town Planning Institute pointed out nervously that this was indeed one of the purposes of planning, and that many people thought it was a very good thing).

---

9 Ibid. (or perhaps op. cit.).

10 Eg Sulkie D. Postcard from geography field trip to Mr and Mrs Sulkie, 15 February 1983.

11 Attrib.

Chief amongst the initiatives were:

- 'Lifting the Burden' (1985)
- 'Building Business – not Barriers' (1986)
- 'Getting Rid of Red Tape' (1987)
- 'Getting Rid of Even More Red Tape, and Then Some' (1988)

They also set in train a permanent process of tinkering with the definition of Permitted Development – a rewarding enterprise that continues to the present day.

In Grotton, at least, none of these strategies seemed to work. Businesses throughout the region continued to close down at a rate which readers may consider unexceptional in today's climate, but which at the time sent shockwaves through the once-proud local economy. Something more radical was needed.

The tone was set by a Mr Nicholas Ridley[12] soon after he was appointed Secretary of State. His address to the annual conference of the National Federation of Housing and Retail Shed Builders on the subject of 'Planners: Who needs 'em?' caused a sensation (the *Daily Telegraph*, for example, lambasted the new minister for his timidity).

The impact of Mr Ridley's appointment was immediate. Suddenly, the Grotton Ring Road – originally built to avoid the place altogether – became nothing more than a handy way of getting to the shops. In total, some eighty-five asbestos-clad boxes now line the Périphérique, as it is known, and at the weekends Ford Foci and Volvi, some with planks of wood sticking out of the window, some with unfortunate cyclists across the bonnet, bring the Spittle i' th' Bottom gyratory to a standstill.

In fact, of course, Ridley's ridicule strengthened the planning profession. People saw what they might be missing if it was lost. Major-General Sir A J C Hartley-Wintergrene, leader of the Dunromin Conservative Party, expostulated in a pamphlet which I have tracked down in my researches that: 'Dunromin will be ruined if we keep allowing things to happen, whatever they are. The whole point of the Conservative Party is to conserve things. We can't go around allowing things to change'.

Some commentators have described the massive increase in unemployment, the creation of vast industrial wastelands and the destruction of whole communities as 'a bit iffy'. But still more misery was to come – local government reorganisation.

In 1986, a complex piece of legislation entitled 'An Act to Abolish the Greater London Council and While We're at it All the Other Metropolitan Counties' passed into law. But it is now clear that the civil servants responsible for drafting it made a fateful mistake. Because Grotton was itself a mistake, it seemed clear that the 1986 Abolition Act could not have applied to it.

How could this possibly have come about? There are three main reasons, but given the fact that my Wordcount Wizard tells me I'm already over my limit, I will move on.

It would seem that when this error was discovered in 1994 there was pandemonium in Whitehall. It was feared that the 1986 Act as a whole might be unlawful, and thus that the GLC might have to be recreated. Fortunately, the matter was rectified by a clause inserted into a schedule to the *VAT (Revocation of Obscure Provisions) (no. 44) (Supply of Services and Chattels) (Miscellaneous) (England) (Amendment) Order 1994*, which was placed in the House of Commons Library on the night when England were losing on a penalty shootout to Liechtenstein.

By 1996, therefore, and just ten years after the abolition of GLC and the other Met Counties, there was no longer a Grotton Metropolitan County Council, there were no metropolitan districts, and everyone just had to make do. New administrative arrangements were hastily put in place (a matter to which I shall return in due course); and the young Treasury solicitor who saved the Government from embarrassment was allowed to retire (at the relatively early age of 23).

Some time ago, readers may recall a reference to the County's Chief Planning Officer, Ted ('T') Break. If there is one man who stands out from the disorientated and disillusioned crowd at that difficult time in Grotton's history, it is not him. But few would dissent from the view that, for ten glorious years, T Break pulled the County up by its bootstraps (an industry Mrs Thatcher had overlooked) and turned it into the powerhouse it became in the 1990s.

T Break's hobby was Scrabble. He belonged to a Coven in Cloggley, and played most nights, once coming ninth at the North West Congregation, and in 1994 he won his junta by three androgynes.

12 Older readers may wish to pour themselves a stiff drink
    at this point.

T Break's winning 1994 Scrabble board

It was about this time that the Government started inventing acronyms (or at least they might easily have been quite acceptable acronyms if they'd just put some decent effort in): UDCs, EZs, DGAs, RDPs, AIDS, DLGs, ABCs, etc. This is a policy which continues to this day and it is one which confuses most people. But T Break was in his element. All his years of training – up at 6.00 every morning for a few lengths of the Board, out in the wind and the rain buying new dictionaries, to the gym every evening for aerobic mathematics – stood him in good stead. He was into every new grant regime before the Manchesters and Birminghams had even drawn breath. He knew more about it than any civil servant and sometimes he made successful bids for programmes that didn't even exist yet.

Break also honed to perfection the different but complementary skills of, on the one hand, presenting to Government and to Europe an overwhelming tale of socioeconomic disadvantage and thus a case for massive financial intervention and, on the other, a persuasive story to potential private sector investors of the county's unparalleled industrial strength and potential.

By 1996, when Ted retired, Grotton had reached new heights – unemployment was down to a historic low of 10%, the treacle was flowing again, the shipyard was back in business making Sony Walkmans, EiP nameplates were in demand. Who at the conference in 1979 could have foreseen this? Planning in Crisis? No! This was Planning in Clover; Planning for Christmas; Planning in Comfort; Planning is Cool.

After the Metropolitan County

So when in 1996 the county finally crept down the slipway of destiny to the graveyard where old administrations are laid to rest, to join Middlesex and the Austro-Hungarian Empire, what happened? Well the county remained as a so-called shire county. The City of Grotton became a unitary authority and the others became shire districts. This is quite normal. Let me explicate.

A brief résumé of the English local government system may help.

There are shire counties (some of which are 'shires' and some not); shire districts (which are bits of shire counties); and unitary authorities. Except in London, which is different. Counties can contain both districts and unitaries, except that the unitaries are not part of the counties for administrative purposes – though they are for geographical purposes. To encourage competition, the boundaries of unitaries are drawn very tightly so they spill over into the other bits of the county. This means that lots of time and money is spent talking about what to do.

Some unitaries are not in counties. They used to be, but the counties were abolished. Some of those were metropolitan counties and some were not, but it doesn't really matter. These unitaries are supposed to work together on what the experts call 'cross boundary issues', or occasionally 'very cross boundary issues', which can essentially be defined as 'everything'. This means that lots of time and money is spent talking about what to do. Sometimes Governments think about reorganising all this but they daren't do it because people absolutely love the old boundaries drawn up 150 years ago when hardly anyone lived in England (even though they don't like anything else about local government), so they tinker about at the edges which makes things worse.

So you might live in a county and also a district, and they share things out between them, or you might live in a unitary which is a kind of hole in a county and does everything as far as it can; or you might live in a unitary, which is just a unitary and not a hole at all but probably makes no functional sense. Or you might live in London, which has to have a mayor (some other places have mayors too, but only if they want to – it's unlikely to help matters if you worry about that too much), and a lot of boroughs, which are a kind of cross between districts and unitaries.

You might also find you live in a parish, which is obviously useful.

I hope this clarifies the situation.

Millennium celebrations at twin town Grôton-sur-mer

But There's a But

The fact of the matter is that, while Governments were fiddling, Grotton was burning. True, there were some successes for a time. The flats overlooking the Blether Navigation initially sold well but now lie idle. The fine new Millennium Concert Hall awaits its first flea market. Treacle has been going through a sticky patch. Nobody even remembers what a Walkman is (the colourful plastic pouches for them were at one time assembled in Cloggley). I won't even mention the EiP nameplates. (Oh, sorry I just did). If it were not for the continued growth of the ~~Polytechnic~~ University (pending) and the consequent demand for bouncers, drug pushers and an army of weekend street cleaners, there would be virtually no economy at all.

But There is Hope

Grotton did not get where it is today without having hope, and already we can taste the green shoots of hope sailing into earshot. The County Council itself has just scored a notable triumph, a triumph which has led directly to this conference, and which looks set to usher in a new age of cautious optimism for the future.

For the Council, after years of introspection and self-doubt, has at last achieved '*average*' in the annual Comprehensive Area Assessment.

As everyone knows, local authorities are marked out of ten every year so people can tell whether they are any good or not. Civilization as we know it could not be maintained without this, and all the time and effort which is spent measuring, calculating, estimating, evaluating and monitoring is clearly well spent. The incredible accuracy of the outcome is a model for the rest of the world.

And, in Grotton's case, the assessors considered that the Council even had '*moderate prospects of remaining average*' (although they did not suggest for how long). It is worth adding that Grotton County Council actually achieved an '*excellent*' rating in some areas – notably in setting up systems for handling complaints, where it is a world leader (though it has to be recognised that it was judged to be '*failing, with little prospect of improvement*' in actually dealing with them).

Within ten short years, the Council has risen from 'moderate' to 'average' – a stunning achievement by any standards. What is the secret of this spectacular success? I have little doubt that there were three main reasons, none of which it seems I have time to describe.

For These Reasons

In order to celebrate this achievement, to raise morale amongst the planners, and to show off Grotton's many attractions (if any), there is to be a new conference – as I may have indicated several pages ago – I haven't time to go back and check.

It was decided to do this in order to mark the thirtieth anniversary of the 1979 Conference. Though this target has been narrowly missed, the thirty-first anniversary is almost as important – arguably more so as 31 is a bigger number than 30 even though it doesn't have a '0' in it. T Break, erstwhile planning supremo and lynchpin of the 1979 Conference is of course no longer in harness, and the heavy mantle of following in his huge shoes has fallen on his successor as Head of Planning at the County, Koffi Break (no relation).

The eyes of the world will be on the delegates, just as they were in 1979. Though, surprisingly, I have not myself been asked to address the conference, I am sure that one or two useful points will come out of the debates. I wish Mr Break, and the delegates, all the luck that they will undoubtedly need.

Despite this lavish landscaping scheme Grotton's cultural quarter is seldom visited

chapter two
The County of Grotton
and the Five Districts of Which it is Comprised of

The City of Grotton

'World city in waiting'

Though the other four Districts may demur, Grotton is clearly the economic and social hub of the county. The services provided by the City make it second only to several other towns in the region.

The city of which Oscar Wilde once said 'Christ, is this it?' has a population which reached a height of 328,362 at the end of the nineteenth century. This had declined by the end of the twentieth to 160,861 according to the 2001 Census (though the City challenged this because they believed it had been printed upside down, and on various other grounds to do with alleged under-representation, specifically of children, students, old people, middle-aged people, men, and women).

Grotton's history has from time immemorial, or thereabouts, been bound up with textiles, with an emphasis on socks, which led to the establishment of Grotton's famous sock exchange (now a Wetherspoons), and corsetry. This provided a firm foundation for the economy for many years, but went out of fashion (other than for certain specialist applications) some time ago.

Textile manufacture relied heavily on cheap labour, of course, and an important feature of the City's history has been the warm welcome it has given over the years to successive waves of immigrant groups. First (if a display in the local history museum is to be believed) it was almost certainly the Cro-Magnons, then a bit later on the Huguenots, followed in more recent times by the Irish, German Jews, West Indians, Kenyan Asians, and Hong Kong Chinese, culminating in a dramatic influx of Poles, Gays and Baristas.[1]

There is no doubt that the 1970s and 1980s were a particularly difficult period for Grotton. During this stressful time, the Council appeared to be unsure of its political direction, allowing itself to be seized by the little-known Real International Revolutionary Marxist Tendency based in Southport. The Grot-Trots, as they were nationally known, set a 'deficit budget',[2] and took steps to secure the establishment of an egalitarian, classless and stateless society based on common ownership and control of the means of production, distribution and exchange. As the administration plunged deeper into debt, the need for a political reality-check became urgent and inevitable. The RIRMT split into nine groups and were never heard of again.

A significant development during this period, however, was the completion in 1989 of the 450,000 sq ft Snodgrass Centre, one of the largest town centre redevelopments of its time, the plans for which had originally been drawn up in 1962. Despite its somewhat unprepossessing appearance, this has been a huge success (except for the concrete cancer, the complete lack of daylight, the malfunctioning air-conditioning system, the fact that there is nowhere to sit down, the empty shop units on the upper level walkways (and the empty maisonettes above them), the unfathomable car-parking arrangements, the fountains which (like fountains everywhere) ceased to function after three days, and the old-age pensioners of Grimethwaite who just come here for the warmth).

---

1 Not to be confused with *barristers* whose contribution to the City's life has been limited to the ostentatious public display of colourful braces.

2 The Government used to say that setting deficit budgets was illegal. That is no longer the case (at least for the Government itself).

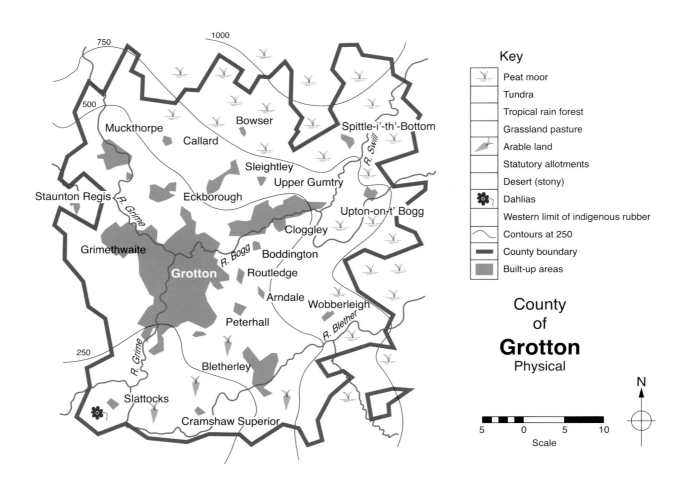

Key

⁂	Peat moor
	Tundra
	Tropical rain forest
	Grassland pasture
⁂	Arable land
	Statutory allotments
	Desert (stony)
✻	Dahlias
	Western limit of indigenous rubber
〜	Contours at 250
▬	County boundary
▨	Built-up areas

County of
Grotton
Physical

N

5   0   5   10
Scale

Of course there is still much to be done. The chronic deficiencies of the City's Victorian transport infrastructure and the crumbling drainage system have remained (an imaginative plan by Will Alsop to solve both of these problems at the same time by suggesting that most trips by private car could be made through the City's principal sewers has been the subject of predictable ridicule).

Local government reorganisation has naturally played a key part in improving the quality of life for residents of the city, and it is something which they have taken to their hearts on a number of occasions. Grotton riotously celebrated becoming a municipal borough in the nineteenth century, then a county borough, then a city, before (in 1974) being awarded fully fledged metropolitan district status. They certainly know how to have a good time in Grotton.

Key

⛵	Shipbuilding (closed)
🧵	Cotton (closed)
🔧	Engineering (closed)
🧦	Socks etc (closed)
⛏	Coal mining (closed)
🪣	Glue (closed)
ZZZ ZZ	Central & local government
🐑	Sheep
🖊	Mainly accountants
$	Banking and commerce
🖥	Nice clean industries
╫	Railway
⁄	Railway (disused)
—	Canal (hardly used)
▨	Built up areas
—	District boundaries
👣	Pennine Way

County
of
Grotton
Political and Economic

N

5   0   5   10
Scale

Thanks in no small part to the unrivalled expertise of Whitehall in masterminding these improvements, the City has now, at long last, achieved the much-prized status of 'unitary authority'. Every authority wants to be unitary, since they think they will be able to do things unitarily. Civil servants find this amusing.

No one believes that this is the last word on reorganisation, or that before too long, Government will fail to take the opportunity of pointing out the obvious deficiencies of the latest arrangements, which it forgot to mention at the time. To begin with, the City's differences with the County Council, which of course (albeit emasculated as we shall see) still exists around the City's boundaries, remain. But they have been limited in recent years to transport, strategic planning, minerals and waste, housing policy, car parking at County Hall, culture and sport, and

Grotton's world famous Mildred Avenue, with its unique layout and its bewildering array of architectural gems

Any Other Business. (The County on the other hand takes the view that the City is too big for its boots, its recent bid to regain control of gas, electricity and defence rather confirming that assessment.)

Meanwhile, of course, the bread-and-butter tasks of preparing development plans, deciding applications and sending burly ex-policemen out to knock down unauthorised conservatories continue as before, although there have naturally been changes at the top since the last conference. Long gone are the days when former City Planning Officer Roland Pratt MIMunE, MICE, Dip TP, FRTPI ruled his department from a cavernous chamber in the Victorian town hall and conducted his never-ending battles with T Break. The most senior planner at the City is now Nicola Tilbrook, the Assistant Chief Executive (Planning and Environment), an energetic young manager, usually to be seen bearing a bottle of still water between meetings or taking a hurried lunch of grass and chopped cabbage from a tupperware box.

Ms Tilbrook oversees the various bits of the planning function, scattered between different Directorates as is the modern fashion (notwithstanding Chief Executive Carol Gibson's enthusiasm for the pursuit of a co-terminous functionality paradigm, going forward). Development Management is in with Environmental Health, located in an annex across the street. Building Control is in a Portakabin behind the Household Waste Recycling Site. Planning Enforcement is combined with a range of other regulatory work including car parking, rat catching, dog wardening and the licensing of lap-dancing clubs, which makes for varied site inspections.

Also under Ms Tilbrook's wing is planning policy. When she was appointed, the Chief Executive made it clear to her that the most important policy as far as she was concerned was that there should be no more than four policies and that, if at all possible, these should not be written down anywhere. This helps to explain why progress on the Local Development Framework for the City has been, at best, patchy.

*The future of Brunel's St Enoch Station
must now be in doubt*

The City projects itself as pursuing a broadly green agenda, despite some reservations from the Chief Executive herself, who wants to see Grotton Ryan Giggs International Airport double in size. Though Nicola opposes this as a matter of principle, its impact would in fact be minimal as the airport has only one flight a week to (or, more accurately, forty miles from) its twin towns of Grottowicze, in Belgium and Grôton-sur-mer, in Poland.

Cloggley

'Doing our best'

Cloggley is a District of contrasts. Dense urban development spreads out from the city along the Bogg Valley in the south west, and wild and windswept moorland covers the north and east. Pretty villages attract commuters, and the local pig farming industry provides them with something to complain about.

Cloggley folk claim that the Industrial Revolution began there – specifically in the hamlet of Upton-on-t'Bogg, on 15 January 1773, in the afternoon. Jedediah Ackroyd finally succeeded in harnessing the power of the turbulent Bogg to operate his three-storey weaving shed, which up to that point had been somewhat nugatory, lacking as it did any form of power other than small children climbing up and down the chimney; this had in fact produced little power, but seemed to be the thing that early industrialists ought to do, and it had at least kept the chimney very clean.

Ackroyd later left Cloggley to set up his great mills at Grotton, where the land was a bit flatter, for the safe operation of his new transverse triple-action thrutching shuttle.[3] Although cotton had been the foundation of the town's success in the nineteenth century, Clogglevians soon went into glue instead, and decided to stick with it.

The glue magnates who brought about this revolution, the McMonocle Brothers, were from a respected Quaker family whose fortune had been built on porridge in Peebles. They chose Cloggley as the base for their new model factory and within two years their main product, Globbo Hygienic Animal Glue ('no needless rats, guaranteed free from domestic pets'), was to be found in every home in the Empire alongside nit powder and Vimto.

In 1987, having been taken over by Anglo–Chinese Adhesives of Shanghai, the Globbo works were the subject of a highly controversial planning application for a 350 foot aluminium-clad giblet sifter. Despite direct action from a local amenity group who glued themselves to the Chinese Consulate in Grotton (on the grounds that the proposed tower would not be in sympathy with the adjacent Italianate offal-grinding shed), permission was granted on appeal. (The tower is now listed and features on the cover of the District tourism brochure.)

Despite its many charms, Cloggley faces a whole host of planning dilemmas. Their sources of bother are quarry owners, rural scrap metal dealers, pig farmers, and stockbrokers from Dunromin who want to convert barns into posh residences (or build new barns for later conversion). The planners have been overwhelmed in recent years as the gentrification of the hill villages has continued apace. Spittle i' th' Bottom, nestling in a fold of the hills by the Swill Brook, has particularly suffered over the last forty years and now displays a range of domestic architectural solutions which, though frequently eye-catching, fail somehow to capture that unity of time and space which local developers, Messrs Bettabuild, have led successive Development Control Committees to expect.

Another difficulty the Borough faces is its relative isolation. Although most residents can hear the M62 from their back gardens, they have to travel at least fifteen miles before they can actually get access to it. It is a similar story with the railway; as recently as 1962 there was a choice of trains to Grotton Sludge Street from Cloggley Central, Cloggley Victoria, and Cloggley High Level (and there was even the odd direct service to Bacup from Cloggley Junction). The Borough still has a railway, but trains now run straight through it without stopping.[4]

But making the best of a bad job has always been Clogglevians' great strength. While Cloggley does not pretend to compete with its more prestigious neighbour down the road, it has begun to nurture its own 'creative industries', based on its unique cultural heritage. The place fairly hums with potters, weavers, tuba players and carbon-neutral Morris dancers. Since 2002, it has also been home to the annual Messiah competition,[5] which draws thousands of visitors to the town every third Thursday after Martinmas.

Peter Rabbit, the amiable Borough Planning and Estates Officer, who joined the Authority in the 1960s, retired in 1991 after a long and happy career. The Council missed him desperately, and when the Leader of the Council discovered that he was alive and well and tending his allotment, he asked him to return to fill the Chief Planner's post ('for old time's sake'), on a temporary contract, until they found someone else. He is still there, and at the age of 79, and supported by statins, is thought to be one of the oldest planning officers still extant.

Peter has always been a fan of the County Council, on the grounds that they have saved him a lot of time and bother looking after tricky things like gypsies, and gravel. He regrets the loss of the Structure Plan, finding that having to make up his own policies on everything is rather taxing. He tries to make as much use as possible of the Regional Spatial Strategy but finds that in relation to things like house extensions it is somewhat lacking in detail. He is a close friend of T Break – they belong to the same Model Railway Society – and still sees him at philatelic evenings where they swap stamps and stories of the old days over a mug of steaming Ovaltine.

Peter has a good relationship with Cloggley's elected members, even though it is what psephologists call a well hung Council.[6] Labour has sixteen, the Lib Dems fourteen and the Conservatives twelve. Five seats are taken by the Independents and one each by the Deep Greens, the Pale Greens, and the Druids. Cloggley being Cloggley, these members fall out in a civilised fashion, over a cup of tea; but nonetheless the shifting alliances between the groups means that layers of gentle chaos frequently prevail. The situation is not helped by a forthcoming by-election following the defection of one of the Labour Members, Geraint Wyn Thomas, to Plaid Cymru.

Cloggley is a member of the 'Considerate Planners' scheme.

---

3 It is interesting to note that the Government has made rapid repetition of this phrase compulsory for all asylum seekers.

4 With the exception of Thomas the Tank Engine, who hauls a Santa Special between Christmas and New Year (normal services are of course suspended during this period on the grounds that too many people want to travel).

5 In 2007, the Sleightley Singers came third, with a time of seven hours, thirty-two minutes, eighteen seconds.

6 Are we sure this is right? Ed.

Dunromin

'Passionate about year on year efficiency savings'

> *Then thread the sunny valley laced with streams*
> *Thro' forests and the o'ershadowed brims*
> *Of simple ponds where idle shepherd dreams*
> *And streaks his restless limbs*

Shelley did not in all probability have the Royal Borough of Dunromin in mind when he wrote these lines,[7] but he might have done. With its verdant pastureland, its stately homes, famous golf courses, public schools and literary connections,[8] Dunromin is at first sight something of an oasis in what is otherwise a pretty ordinary former Metropolitan County.

The prime focus is Bletherley, a rapidly growing town which sees itself more as part of distant Surrey than as part of anything so inconvenient as 'north west England'. The locals vehemently resist any suggestion that they have anything in common with their less refined neighbours, still less that they are dependent on the rest of Grotton for anything other than employment (though in fact only 8% of the population actually work within Dunromin), transport, entertainment, culture, sport, and a few other things.

Dunromin is quick to point to the ancient origins of Bletherley itself, though to the casual visitor little evidence exists of the alleged medieval core. Thanks to the large scale redevelopment of the 1970s, all that remains from earlier times is a plaque marking the original site of the market cross, a branch of Coutts Bank in the old Bletherley Literary and Philosophical Society (itself substantially rebuilt in the Georgian style in 1959), and an air raid shelter from the Second World War.

The dull shopping arcade which was built at that time was the brainchild of the Council Leader of the day, Major-General Sir A J C Hartley-Wintergrene (dec'd). His son, Sir Hartley Hartley-Wintergrene, has had the task of overseeing its replacement and a brand new white elephant with tiresomely predictable retail outlets now stands in its place. The centre, which is locked at night to prevent people getting from one side of Bletherley to the other, also comes complete with security guards to chuck out people who are not spending enough.

It cannot compete, however, with the jewel in Dunromin's retail crown – Prince Regent Avenue, with its hanging baskets and big round things in the middle of the pavement for you to bump into and try and sue the Council over because you stubbed your toe. Here, if you need a Dolce & Gabbana thong or a time-share in Barbados, you are fine – though lavatory paper and packets of fish fingers are only to be had by special order (or by sneaking into Morrisons out on the bypass). Due to the nation's economic meltdown (which many of Bletherley's residents had a hand in), it also has some of the best-stocked charity shops in the country.

Dunromin welcomes hot food takeaways which meet their exacting design criteria

---

7 Shelley, in fact, didn't write them at all.

8 Mrs Gaskell's husband, Mr Gaskell, used to train his whippets near Bletherley.

A frequent winner of Keep Britain Tidy's Best Best Kept Village Competition, the Royal Borough has seventy-nine Conservation Areas (many of which overlap), and there are some 200 active Civic and Amenity Societies, ranging from the Friends of Bletherley to Dunromin Residents Opposed to Just About Anything, to Dunromin Residents Opposed to Just About Anything Else, and Friends of the Lake District (where many Dunromin residents have second homes).

For a time, the Lib Dems caught the Borough's imagination with their campaign slogan *Tell us What You Want, What You Really Really Want*, resulting in their being swept to power in the election of 2003. Their popularity did not last, however, mainly because most of the things it turned out people really, really wanted were illegal. The Conservatives have now reclaimed what they see as their rightful place at the head of the Borough's affairs.

At the time of the last conference the Chief Planner was the mercurial Nigel Smoothe. Never having blotted his copybook for the whole of his twenty-eight years' service with the Council, he was given the benefit of a generous early retirement package (subject to the usual requirement not to speak to the press), and went to live on the south coast with his former secretary and a small dog, occasionally emerging in a low-key, background sort of a way to offer some helpful observations to the House Builders Federation.[9]

Dunromin's Georgian heritage arrives on the back of a lorry

These days, ensuring that planning activity in Dunromin maintains the high standards which its residents demand is the responsibility of the Chief Executive, Jeremy Sheene. A former England Rugby International (one cap against Japan), Sheene had several years of experience in investment banking. He was headhunted by Dunromin, who actually believed that his City experience and management expertise in the banking sector might be useful. Sheene entered the Authority with the intention of changing everything. His favourite motivational jingle is *If You're Happy in Your Work, Something's Wrong*. This provides the key to understanding his frenetic commitment to the implementation, throughout the Council's services, of Advanced Continuous Chaos Theory, something he'd picked up on his MBA course at Harvard.

'Managing Change Management' had been the theme of his thesis, and the material he had copied from the internet for that purpose had led him to the view that so long as nothing remained the same for more than a few minutes all would be well. Every couple of months he reorganises the Authority, giving all the departments imprecise names and disjointed functions, and, crucially, dispensing with most of the Chief Officers. His consummate skill in creating an impression of continuous and decisive action has led to his being awarded the Institute of Transformational Outcomes Gold Medal.

Sheene delegates the less important aspects of planning to Barbara Turpentine, a third tier officer with great ability and little power. Though she attends meetings about policy matters, her instruction is to say and do nothing about anything important without Sheene's personal approval.

There is no real planning strategy in the District other than the need to stop anything happening. That and the perennial difficulty of ensuring that anything that does get built fully respects the sensitive neo-Georgian traditions of the town. Developers have made many attempts over the years to nibble away at the Green Belt (the boundaries of which are drawn very tightly around Bletherley and its satellite villages); but Dunrominians, especially those whose delightful homes occupy plots which were themselves in the Green Belt until very recently, can always be relied upon to defend to the death the quality of life that they are uniquely equipped to appreciate.

9 Now the much more cuddly 'Home Builders Federation' apparently.

Dunromin receives very large numbers of planning applications, and employs as few people as possible to deal with them. Its twin aims are to preserve the character of the District, and to deal with casework at an ever faster rate. It has long been in the forefront of innovative techniques to achieve at least a 100% record in meeting its eight-week targets. It has perfected the essential skill of 'delayed registration', and its process for routinely sending applications back and asking for further information is now of course standard across most Authorities.

The Council encourages applicants to withdraw many perfectly satisfactory applications after 7½ weeks, and re-submit them. According to Jeremy Sheene this '… *allows us to cascade downstream some of the key customer outputs so that they can be re-baselined at a later point in the development cycle*'.

Unsurprisingly, given that only 23% of applications are approved, there is a very large number of appeals in Dunromin, the majority of which it loses. The overturning of 45% of officers' recommendations does not assist in this regard. This has been the subject of some criticism in the press, especially when the Council refused the ~~Polytechnic~~ University (pending) of Central Grotton permission to extend a Hall of Residence in Cramshaw Superior on the grounds that 'it would lower the tone of the neighbourhood, contrary to the wishes of the electorate'. The Ward Councillor was quoted as saying that the Planning Inspector's decision to award costs of £450,000 against the Council was 'simply the price of democracy'.

Grimethwaite

'Mission impossible'

What can be said about Grimethwaite that has not already been recorded in countless geography textbooks, Channel 4 documentaries, and decisions by the Ombudsman? Exactly.

It is hard to imagine that only 200 years ago the Grime was a clear and swiftly flowing river, the finest for salmon south of the Ribble. For not since 1878, when a solitary frog was seen gasping for breath at Muckthorpe Bottoms, has anything fallen into those waters and lived.

Sadly, despite a major regeneration effort, the Borough still displays a bewildering concentration of environmental disasters. Eighty-three percent of the area is taken up with spoil tips, waste dumps, clay pits and redundant sewage works; and derelict railways, cotton mills, chemical works and charity shops make up much of the remainder. Most of the houses lack basic amenities (22%, for example, have no wide screen television). Fortunately, as a result of heavy local demand, the disinfectant industry still thrives (carbolic soap was first synthesised in Muckthorpe in 1919), but even that is a shadow of its former self.

There is undoubtedly a feeling of defeat about Grimethwaite. No one seems to care any more – in fact when the Government recently announced that a vast area to the west of Muckthorpe was to be used as a tip for spent nuclear fuels, only three people signed a petition, and one of those was in favour.

Local people have a saying 'Wur th's muck i' th' grittlin', yer'll nobbut get tha' weftin' treddled', and while that's as true now as ever it was, it just doesn't seem to help any more. Matters have been made worse over the years by the fierce and loveless rivalry between Grimethwaite and Muckthorpe. Back in 1973 the two towns had even found it impossible to agree what the new metropolitan authority should be called (Grimethwaite had favoured 'Grimethwaite', whereas Muckthorpe, its smaller rival, preferred 'Muckthorpe'). The Secretary of State of the day, being a busy man who had never heard of either place, had thumbed through his RAC handbook and, finding Grimethwaite displayed in the bolder type, settled on that as the name for the new entity. It was only by chance that the reorganised authority avoided being called 'Page 127, K3'.

Grimethwaite is the only major retail centre in the country anchored by a Sue Ryder shop. This is because, in the 1980s, the Council decided to encourage something called 'a retail-led regeneration initiative' out near the deserted link road to the M62. Equidistant from both Grimethwaite and Muckthorpe, a key objective of the Grimeside Mall (which was said to have the largest roof in the far south eastern part of the north west) is to prevent 'leakage' of expenditure from one town centre to the other, and vice versa. This is what a series of eminent consultants had advised the Council to do, and it demonstrates that you can prove anything with figures.

More recently, the 'World of Waste' theme park has been very much more successful. Playing to Grimethwaite's strengths, the theme park is a trail-blazing attraction which, through practical demonstrations and interactive electronic displays, tells the story of rubbish. According to its publicity leaflets (which themselves make up a fair proportion of the waste produced in the Borough), 'there's something for all the family'. Children can help sort through piles of refuse and take out useful bits of metal. Mums can fashion clothing from discarded bin liners. Dads can help by going around Council Estates and emptying the bins, and an animatronic Borough Engineer tells the story of how cardboard can be recycled to make pizza.

Buoyed by the success of the dustcart dodgems, the Council has recently commissioned consultants to report on the feasibility of introducing more Disney-style rides with an environmental theme, such as 'Mutants of the Caribbean' and 'It's a Small, Small Planet'. Members have however been very much put off by the specifics of the Splash Mountain proposal.

Ron Blunt, the former amateur car breaker and Chief Planner of Grimethwaite, was the power behind the theme park. Unfortunately he was killed at the opening when a refuse truck reversed over him during a demonstration of the latest dustcart technology. Cllr Sid Spriggs, the firebrand Leader of the Council (which is politically split, rather acrimoniously, between thirty-nine Old Labour Members and one New Labour) and former President of the Amalgamated Carbolic Soap, Talc and Aromatherapy Operatives Union, immediately appointed Wayne Blunt – Ron's son – in his place. Wayne had started out as a technician and worked his way up: Grimethwaite was in his blood (which of course meant that he suffered from a range of interesting diseases, many of them unique to the District). Actually born under an ASBO, Wayne retained his father's

antipathy to the County Council. The abolition of Structure Plans in 2004 was celebrated with a mass sacrifice of copies of the Plan in Muckthorpe Park – unfortunate, really, as many of its policies were to remain in force for a number of years.

The Council has not lost a single appeal in the last five years. Cllr Spriggs initially thought that this was something worth celebrating: however, a maths graduate, taken on as a planning technician, has since pointed out that the Council's appeal record is not 100% as the Leader thought, but infinity. Since they never refuse planning permission, they hadn't won any appeals either.

The Council's overwhelmingly positive approach to development in the Borough is also exemplified by the speed with which they issue their decisions. In most cases, they are able to issue a notice of approval within eight minutes of receiving the application (and the all-important cheque); for a small extra fee, applicants have the option to impose their own conditions; and there are regular 'Buy One, Get One Free' promotions for priority application categories such as global headquarters for pharmaceutical conglomerates and call centres for Indian credit card companies. Such applications are all too rare. In fact non-existent.

Grimethwaite has recently made a bid to host a series of I'm a Celebrity – Get Me Out of Here.

Golden Delicious – a general view

Golden Delicious

*'All our operatives are
engaged on other calls'*

Huddled inconspicuously at the south western extremity of the fertile Grotton Plain,[10] which still mercifully separates the County from Greater Manchester, lies Golden Delicious. Based on the rather less romantic sounding settlement of Slattocks, Golden Delicious was simply a leftover. It seems that the Boundary Commission were exhausted from dealing with the good folk of Bletherley (who, as we have seen, never wanted to be part of Greater Grotton in the first place, and were especially keen to have nothing to do with places like Slattocks where people may not fully appreciate the qualities which Dunromin aspired to espouse). Confused by the pre-war motoring maps from which they had been working, they committed a fateful error. Even to

the casual visitor the sense of isolation is immediately apparent, and nobody doubts that it would probably be better for all concerned if Golden Delicious had never been created. This is understood to be the view of the District Council itself.

In reality there is some historical justification for this separation. Its ancient name was 'The Soke of Slattocks', and its position at the confluence of the Grime and the Blether gives it a degree of strategic insignificance remarkable even by Grotton standards. It is almost famous for dahlias. Two miles south of Slattocks there is a roche moutonnée. Or it could be a drumlin. The church of St Rita is said to have the poorest acoustics in England.

10 Student planners are directed to look at
    the bottom left-hand corner of the map.

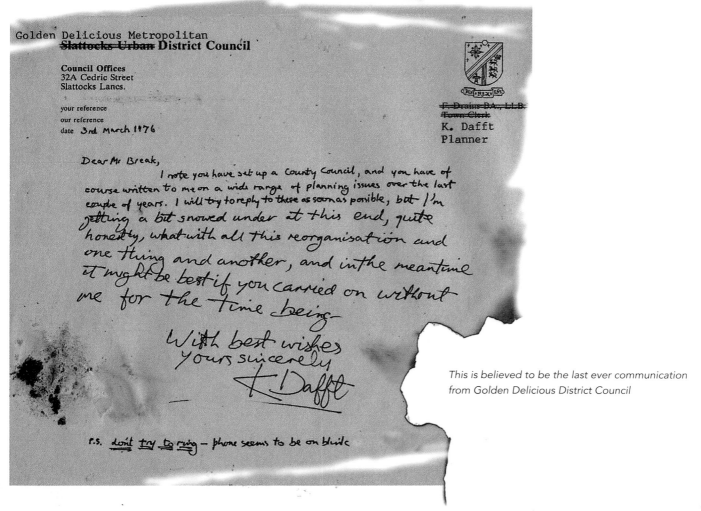

This is believed to be the last ever communication
from Golden Delicious District Council

Despite an obvious case for its abolition, successive reviews of the local government structure have left Golden Delicious unusually untouched. This is not for want of trying, but not one of the surrounding Authorities has been willing to take it on. Having never got round to joining the Local Government Association, and absent as it always seems to be from any meetings organised on anything by the Government Office for the Region, and untouched as it is by any of the activities of the Royal Town Planning Institute, the Planning Advisory Service, or the Sunday Times Wine Club, Golden Delicious feels more unnecessary than ever.

Ken Dafft, who was in charge of planning at the time of the 1979 Conference, has never been seen since. Indeed he was never seen at the time. There is still an office at 32a Cedric Street, over a betting shop just across the floral roundabout from the Slattocks and Stubbins Joint Equitable and Industrial Co-operative Society's funeral parlour, which bears the name 'Dafft'. Recent work carried out there by archaeologists from the ~~Polytechnic~~ University (pending) has yielded a small leather suitcase (empty), a biro removed from a hotel in Prestatyn (dysfunctional), a pair of Wellington boots (muddy), a jam sandwich (mouldy), and a bronze goblet dating from the third century BC.

Dafft himself, however, remains elusive. The *Grotton Advertiser* recently produced a feature article to commemorate his unexplained disappearance almost 31½ years ago, bringing together all the most plausible theories. There are photographs of a possible sighting in Valparaiso; and there is the particularly intriguing discovery of a pair of check trousers on a beach at Cleethorpes.

It is therefore no surprise that letters sent to 32a Cedric Street are returned with the handwritten endorsement from the weary local postman, '*How many times do we have to tell you: NOT KNOWN AT THIS ADDRESS!*' A recorded message on the only number available through Directory Inquiries gives the slightly ominous advice, 'Overall you'd be well advised not to call this number again', while any attempt to access the Council website offers, 'Oops, this link appears to be broken. Did you mean Goldendelicious.apple.mac?'

It is understood that any planning applications are decided by the Duckworth–Lewis method.

Ken Dafft – the last known picture

Grotton County Council

'Could have been worse'

The diversity and heterogeneity of the County of Grotton will have been obvious from these accounts of the Districts of which it is comprised. 'Variety' is its other name. From the sumptuous plains of Dunromin, through the majestic City of Grotton itself, to the lofty hills of Cloggley, via the awesome opencast mines of Muckthorpe and the magisterial flower beds of Golden Delicious, there truly is something for everybody.

After the 1996 reorganisation, it took the County Council some time to come to terms with its diminished responsibilities. Eventually it found out what these were, and now carries them out as well as could possibly be expected. Last year it submitted futile comments on over 600 consultation documents, which broke its previous record by nearly 100.

The glory days of ex-Chief T Break (who so narrowly missed qualifying for the quarter finals of the 1977 RTPI Most Promising Middle-Aged Planner award), and his formidable department, are gone. Every year, however, on 1 April (which is the anniversary of the adoption of the first great Structure Plan), the ageing T Break comes out from his retirement in a bungalow in Upton-on-t'Bogg for a quiet staff reunion and celebration. The members of his once great team of all the talents from '79 are of course invited along. Al Gebbra, the mathematical wizard behind the Analysis of Inter-Connected Decision Areas[11] – which, it will be recalled, involved weeks in front of vast charts in the Weighting Room in the basement of County Hall measuring, modelling and manipulating things – is usually unable to attend, but sends his laptop in his place. Euthanasia Proode, Break's former Secretary, is also absent on most occasions, due to her flatulence, and former Head of Development Control Ernest Quill and the old Admin Chief Gerald Piles generally have other things to do.

Ex-Council Leader Alderman Grimshaw rarely leaves his Sunset Home these days, where he is frequently visited by former Council officers who have not yet plucked up the courage to inform him that he no longer runs the Authority. So T Break celebrates the old County's myriad achievements quietly with Mrs Break; a visit to the Country Cottage Tearooms followed by a small firework display and the annual attempt at sexual intercourse always cheers him up.

Iberian autocracy – the imposing El Sub-sta

11 AIDA was a well known and much misunderstood technique for endlessly analysing alternative options in a scientific way in order to come up with the answer you had already thought of. And an opera.

Planning at the County Council is now part of the Department of Transport and Environment, which was fashioned from the amalgamation of the old 'Planning', 'Highways and Transportation', and 'Word Processing' teams. These three departments had always had a close interdependency and working relationship with each other – except for Highways and Transportation obviously – and now work in harmony, of a sort, under the formidable Donald MacDonald.

Donald has been with Grotton for much of his life, and before the reorganisation was the County Surveyor and Bridgemaster. At 62, he would like to retire; but he is held in such high regard that his requests have been declined. He took on his extra responsibilities with some reluctance. Not for him the niceties of sustainable development – his life had revolved around steel and concrete. His grandfather built the Forth Bridge and the Clachnacuddin Transporter. His father widened the M5 and bypassed Wrexham. His mother dug the Mersey Tunnel. And now Donald has found not only that his engineering role has been reduced to the odd pelican crossing and cycle path, but he has to grapple with planning too.

Fortunately of course most of this is now a District function, with the County dealing mainly with minerals and waste. Both of these, involving as they do big trucks and diggers, blasting and scraping, gouging and boring, get the adrenaline going as they did for his ancestors before him.

But Donald has found, through AGA (the Association of Grotton Authorities: Motto: *AGA CAN*), that he has had little choice but to become involved in wider planning matters, and it is a tribute to his good sense and fearsome personality that he has been asked to Chair AGA–POG (the AGA Planning Officers Group). Surprised to find himself regarded as a peacemaker, Donald now almost enjoys the role. Deals are struck, unholy alliances are forged, Rover Assorted are nibbled – and, just occasionally, if Wayne Blunt is present, drinks might be thrown.

Since Donald finds the nitty-gritty of planning itself a bit of a scunner, which can readily get him into a fankle, he leaves it to Koffi Break, who sits at third tier in the department. Among his other duties, Koffi stands in for Donald when there's a potentially hostile public meeting to attend.

It is to the T and E Department that much of the burden of maintaining the County Council's hard won status of 'Average and with Moderate Prospects of Remaining Average' will fall, and it is to Koffi that Donald has inevitably turned to organise the major Planning in Crisis 2010 Conference.

Cloggley used to be famous for carrots

The Government Office

'Here to help'
(subject to changes in Government policy)

Alexander Quibble, Regional Director of the Government Office (GO), has not been in post long. Gone are the days when people like N Cumbrance – who was in charge at the time of the 1979 Conference – would remain in post for years and get to know the area.[12] Actually knowing relevant things is not regarded as important in the modern Civil Service (though knowing irrelevant things is highly prized, as is not knowing that irrelevant things are in fact irrelevant).

Quibble came from the Home Office, where he had worked on the annual 'Even Tougher on Crime than the Last Act' Act, a tradition which has been in train for thirty years. Before that he was in the Treasury, the Foreign Office, International Development, Energy, Health, and Education Departments. Quibble is 32.

Naturally he has no knowledge of planning. In this he differs not at all from any of his colleagues in the GO and indeed most of his colleagues in Eland House, the Headquarters of 'Communities and Local Government', as it is currently known. (It is very likely that by the time the Planning in Crisis Conference takes place it will have changed its name several times. The bookies' favourites at the time of going to press were 10/1 Local Government and Communities; 33/1 Ministry of Housing and Local Government; and 100/1 the compromise Department of Environment, Planning, Transport, Sustainable Development and National Regional Urban Suburban and Rural Affairs.)

Despite this almost total ignorance of the subject it is from Eland House and Dan Smith House, Grotton (home of the GO, and a veritable hive of inactivity) that planning is now micromanaged. Step by tiny step, over the thirty years since 1979, civil servants with the best of intentions and the worst of competences have involved themselves in the affairs of Grotton in ways which T Break in his heyday would have found inconceivable, but which to Koffi Break are the norm.

It is here in Dan Smith House that the hotly contested British record was established for the longest time ever taken to decide whether to call something in. At nearly five years, this is a record which is unlikely to stand for very long.

However the record for the most unhelpful comment on a local plan ('in policy E276 line 2, insert the word *normally*') was later beaten by the South West office ('in policy H937 line 7, delete the word *normally*').

It was also from here that a leaflet entitled, '*Your Grotton. Your Services. Your Leaflet*' was recently issued, which could render much of the foregoing null and, indeed, void. It appears to signal the Government's interest in another round of restructuring. More details may well emerge at the conference itself, but it seems that the options being canvassed are four:

1. to abolish the five districts and form a single unitary authority called 'Grotton'
2. to abolish the County, for the City to remain unitary, and the other four districts to merge to form a second unitary called 'Golden Dunclogthwaite' or 'Grotton Without'
3. as 2, but for Grimethwaite and Cloggley to form a single unitary and Dunromin to merge with Cheshire East (the position with respect to Golden Delicious being left until the next reorganisation)
4. as 3, but Dunromin to merge with Tuscany

No doubt in 2041, when a further conference will presumably be held to celebrate the thirty-first anniversary of this one, and Grotton will perhaps achieve 'passable' in the annual performance assessments, the authors will be brought out of retirement to produce a further book in this series (in very large print). That will provide an opportunity to bring the reader up to date.

12 Sir Norman retired when it became obvious he was past it, and now holds a number of Directorships in the City.

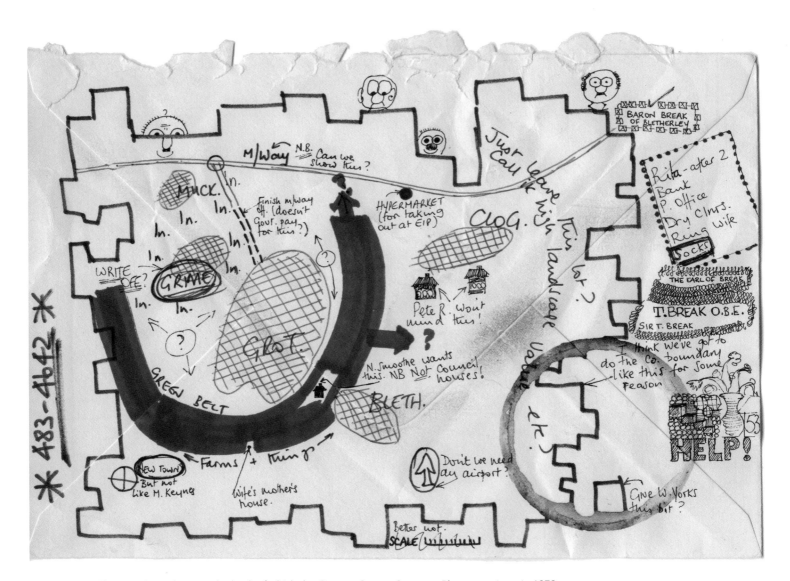

The actual envelope on the back of which the Grotton County Structure Plan was written in 1979

chapter three

The Development Plan in Crisis

Introduction
– So What is the Development Plan Exactly?

Put simply, a development plan is something in accordance with which any determination under the Planning Acts, where regard is to be had to it, has to be, unless material considerations indicate otherwise. Another way of putting it is that a development plan is something where, if any determination has to have regard to it (that is, the development plan), it (that is, the determination) has to be made in accordance with it (the development plan), unless (as before) material considerations indicate otherwise. Now let's get on.

In 2007, Koffi Break, on behalf of AGA, wrote to Alexander Quibble at the Government Office (GO) for the region to ask him to explain the not-all-that-new development plan system. Quibble's reply, when it eventually came, deserves to be better known. The system has heretofore defied comprehensible explanation, but extracts from his letter should greatly assist in dealing with some of the grey areas which persist. Mr Quibble has been asked to speak at the Planning in Crisis Conference in 2010, though having been in post in Dan Smith House for nearly two years it is likely that by then he will have moved to pastures new, bringing his undoubted talent to bear on some other subject of which he has no particular knowledge.

The Regional Plan

Mr Quibble's exposition on the Development Plan system began as follows (see overleaf):

GOVERNMENT OFFICE FOR THE NORTH WEST

Incorporating MHLG, DOE, DETR, DTLR, ODPM, CLG, DfT, DECC,
whatever DBERR is called now, defra and possibly a few others

GROTTON REGIONAL OFFICE
DAN SMITH HOUSE, BACK SIDE STREET WEST, GROTTON GR11 9ZX

Ref: NW/GROT/AQ/P60
23 February 2008

Modernising the Planning System

Dear Mr Break

Thank you so much for your letter of 2 January 2007. I am sorry for the delay in replying but as you will appreciate I am somewhat overwhelmed with important business in my vital role here at the Government Office. It must also be said that your request on behalf of AGA for an explanation of the Development Plan system was a difficult one. My colleague, Mr Albatross, has had to carry out extensive research. However I am sure that what follows will enable your constituent Authorities to proceed with all speed towards the successful preparation of a "Development Plan".

a) National Planning Policy

You did ask me to say a word about planning at the national level. This of course, insofar as we engage in it, does not form part of the development plan, and it is not the subject of Inquiries, Examinations and the like. I think you can take it, therefore, that our policies are, by definition, unimpeachable.

However, if it helps, I was talking to the Minister only last night and I can say that the Government is determined that London and the south east, with its successful financial services industries and expensive restaurants, should continue to grow and develop unfettered by regulation or inhibition. Our expectation is that the success of these industries – where we are of course world leaders - will "trickle down" (as our very expert economists put it) to regions such as your own. Unfortunately this is currently subject to review.

We do have, of course, a proud record in infrastructure planning at national level. The National Policy Statements which will emerge as a result of the 2008 Act are certain to be crystal clear, as I am sure you will accept, and our consultation processes are the very envy of the civilised world; the various challenges which I am told may ensue in the Courts are a mere irritant with little chance of success.

b) The Regional Spatial Strategy

I deal now with the "Regional Spatial Strategy", a document which, as its name implies, is a strategy for the Region of which Grotton forms such a small but nonetheless large part.

I

You will, I am sure, recall that for many years planners were instructed that regional planning was of no value whatsoever. Your colleague in Cloggley, Mr Robot, may remember that in the 1960s and 70s a number of plans were produced and it seems that against all the odds these set an effective framework for planning in the Region for many years. This is not something which my colleagues in CLG had previously appreciated. Despite this, as a Civil Servant representing the former Mr Heseltine may have said at your conference in 1979 (though as all copies of his speech have been lost, I can't be sure), the Government of the day decided to do without regions altogether – but after a while they realised that this approach had its shortcomings, and indeed made sensible planning almost impossible. They introduced something called Regional Planning Guidance (which was only "guidance" in the mandatory sense of the word), and this became the Regional Spatial Strategy (RSS) in 2004. A sound statutory and democratic basis for RSS was achieved by asking the Regional Assemblies to have a go at preparing them.

RSSs have now been in operation for four years. It is not often that the Government allows a part of the planning system to remain unaltered for so long without proposing to change it. In some ways this is a tribute to the work of the Regional Assemblies. The fact that it took longer for the plans to be approved by us than it did to prepare them in the first place is entirely because of the assiduousness with which we engaged with the process, and in no way due to any lack of competence, decisiveness or expertise on our part.

You will be aware of the establishment of the Department for Business, Enterprise and Regulatory Reform (known as DBERR). As the last part of its name implies, it has been given the necessary and important job of reforming regulations, which will no doubt occupy it for many years.[1] I am aware that your colleagues in AGA have questioned this, saying firstly that there seems no need to alter something which seems to be working quite well; and secondly that they are finding it hard to keep up with all these changes. I would like to address these two points which, if I may say so, display a surprising degree of naivety.

Firstly, altering regulations is what we know about here in the corridors of power. You can rest assured that we are world leaders in this field. Whilst we respect, to a degree, the views of your colleagues, I think on the whole your strengths, such as they are, lie in dealing expeditiously with any planning application which might come your way, rather than getting involved in these more complex matters. As to your second whinge, it is, if I may say so, futile and indeed anachronistic to grumble about "change". Your colleagues need to understand that this is now the norm.

I would add that we did of course consult widely on these improvements. I understand that in this instance there was not a unanimity of view. A number of supposedly well informed bodies such as the self-styled "Royal Town Planning Institute" expressed reservations about the proposals, referring to things like a "democratic deficit"; it seems that they think that the Regional Development Agencies (RDAs, who are to take over Regional Planning, sorry about all these initials!!) suffer from this alleged deficiency, due mainly to the complete absence of any electoral process. They overlook, of course, the lack of democratic accountability of the Assemblies themselves (Note to self – how come we thought they were OK in 2004?).

However we have not been deflected from our chosen course by such insubstantial complaints, and anyway, as the Minister pointed out to me only recently, we have re-invented the Assemblies in another form, called a Leaders' Board. Though it is true that these may become a source of dissent and delay, there will always be doubters and naysayers, and I think it is our duty to press forward in the interests of good Governance, and in any event, clearly it will in no way be the fault of HM Government if the Leaders of all the Local Authorities cannot agree these matters amongst themselves.

I am told that a future Government may decide to do away with regional planning altogether, but of course it will only be a matter of time before it has to be reinvented yet again.

I hope this is helpful. I am grateful for your interest in this particularly elusive aspect of the system, and for the fact that you did not ask me to define the word "spatial" …

II

---

1 The department was abolished shortly afterwards.

Mr Quibble's letter went on to deal with other parts of the process, and his thoughts will be of value later. But first, a summary of regional planning in Grotton to date …

How was the Regional Spatial Strategy Produced, Then?

The Regional Assembly had consulted on a draft RSS in early 2006. The Grotton Authorities were naturally among those who responded and extracts from their letters to the Assembly may help to sum up the situation in their own words:

City of Grotton

Nicola Tilbrook BA DipTP MRTPI
Assistant Chief Executive – Planning and Environment
Town Hall
Grotton GR1 1AA

GROTTON
CITY COUNCIL

28 Feb 2006

Dear Derek

Regional Spatial Strategy

While we realise that you are obliged to prepare an RSS, what I think my members would want to stress is that here at the City of Grotton we do have things well under control as far as planning's concerned, and so we see only a limited role for the Strategy in practice. Its main purpose will obviously be to ensure that anything useful that happens in the Region will happen in Grotton. We have ambitious plans for growth, expecting by the middle of the century to rival Manchester and Liverpool. So long as you recognise the scope for retail, employment and housing development on brownfield land, and provide clear support for the casino, opera house, new stadium, branch of the Tate, media city, eco-town, new docks, Freeport, high speed railway line, light rapid transit system, park and ride sites, Olympic sized swimming pool and synchronised swimming facility, 'Green' initiative, new terminal and runway, new shopping development in the 'Car Boot' quarter, industrial park, and redevelopment of Dan Smith House, we are unlikely to have any real concerns.

Unfortunately we do have to object to some specifics, if they are still in your minds, in particular the retail policies (which could lead to the move of the football stadium from Cowpat Park to Muckthorpe), and we hope you will deal swiftly with Dunromin's objections to the proposed park and ride site which lies within its boundaries. We expect to be self-sufficient in waste soon, though we note that Grimethwaite would like some rubbish for their theme park and we are sure we can co-operate in that respect.

We are of course a Unitary Authority so we expect to be invited to take the leading role at the EiP.

Yours,

Nicola Tilbrook

Nicola

Nicola Tilbrook's letter on the RSS

GRIMETHWAITE BOROUGH COUNCIL
Town Planning Department | Town Hall | POBox 22
Muckthorpe | Near Grotton

W BLUNT | CHIEF PLANNER

25 April 2006

Del

We note that the RSS proposes that no new houses should be built in our area due to lack of demand. However we wonder whether it might be possible to provide for a nice new semi, or maybe even a pair. We are short of more upmarket property. Cllr S Spriggs, the Council Leader, has written to me to say (and I quote): 'We are frankly tired of being treated as a dumping ground for whatever places like Dunromin don't want. This is discrimination. What about the workers? How can we turn Grimethwaite around when this class-ridden planning system foists yet more of your so-called densification on us? What does Lord Rogers know about Muckthorpe, middle class posho prat?'

We have of course a very large quantity of brownfield land – in fact almost all the Borough falls into that category, and we would like to see something done about it. Is there any money in it?

W Blunt

W Blunt

Wayne Blunt's response on behalf of Grimethwaite

Cloggley District Council

Planning and Public Health Section
P. Rabbit
Borough Planning and Estates Officer (temp) (ret'd)
Elsie Street
Cloggley GR47 8QZ

19 March 2006

My Dearest Derek

Re: The regional business

Firstly I must apologise for the late reply to your consultation letter, which went by accident to the Head of Development Control and was registered as a planning application. Can you believe it?! She came to me complaining about the lack of information and precision in the key diagram (which had no north point, for example, and only the sketchiest outline of your proposals), and recommended that we return it with a request for further information. Fortunately I had time to read the accompanying letter and I realised her mistake; the division is as you will understand under a lot of pressure.

Happily your proposed RSS seems to be an excellent document and I congratulate you on the hard work you have obviously put into it. Very well done indeed.

However, we note a very high number of houses proposed for the District. In a situation where Upper Gumtry has already grown by nearly 30% in the last six months, and is beginning to lose its historic character as a result, I wonder if this is really fair? I sometimes think that our willingness to keep out of your way in your extraordinarily difficult task may be working against us, though as you know I would never accuse you of trying to take advantage of us, since I am sure that you work to the highest professional standards. Nonetheless, I do note that the Royal Borough of Dunromin next door has a very much lower allocation. I hope you will be able to address this point, and I am sorry to be a nuisance.

I must say I quite like those nice new wind farms – they can be seen for miles and really enhance the Pennines.

Good luck!!!

Very best wishes

Peter

Peter

PS Could I enter just a small objection to the Sleightley Orbital Ring Road, which seems to pass very close to my mother-in-law's place?

Peter Rabbit's response on behalf of Cloggley

Office of the Chief Executive
JEREMY SHEENE MBE MA (Oxon) FRICS FIBA FIMS ACCA
Civic Centre, Prince Regent Square
Bletherley GR9 5AY

Royal Borough of

Dunromin

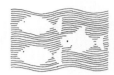

4 May 2006

<u>"Regional Spatial Strategy"</u>

Dear Mr Dougan

We would very much prefer that you did not indulge in this orgy of plan making. We are aware that there is provision in the statutes for an 'RSS', but we see no reason for the undue haste you have shown in rushing to produce it. We think it is an affront to local democracy that a body such as yours, lacking electoral legitimacy, and dealing with a region so large as this one, has produced in a mere matter of months a 'strategy' which could be perceived as affecting the residents of the Royal Borough. I am instructed by the Leader of the Council to remind you that it is a commitment by the Conservative Party nationally to abolish the North West of England and all that it stands for.

In particular we note that you propose that a large number of 'houses' should be built in our area. We can see no need for this and we demand that those proposals are withdrawn. We are even more outraged that some of those are described as being 'affordable'. In our case, as you know, the whole character of the Royal Borough is based on the fact that our housing stock is unaffordable. This helps to maintain the quality of the environment and is the social adhesive which holds our community together. We may be prepared to permit a few executive houses in parts of the area, but no more, and we will certainly not contemplate the unappetising prospect of what you call 'high density brownfield' development which would be quite out of place here. We are not in favour of over-regulation; but nobody in the Royal Borough is going to want their neighbours to be able to build all over their back gardens, especially where it might prevent them from doing the same in due course.

In any event, my Leader wishes me to add that the population and household forecasts on which your 'strategy' is based are clearly faulty, and that if it wasn't for the number of immigrants there would not be a problem. He believes they should all be sent back home. We will adduce evidence on this point at the appropriate time.

We also object strongly to the proposed park and ride site in our area, which is completely out of keeping with our rural surroundings; in any event our residents wish to drive into Grotton and park cheaply there, rather than suffer the inconvenience of having to get out of their cars and ride on a 'bus', and we demand that you base your policies on this principle. We also wish to see expenditure allocated as a matter of priority to extra lanes on the Grotton ring road. Those of our residents who have second homes in the Lake District are finding access to the M62 on Friday afternoons to be increasingly difficult and obviously this is a problem which needs to be addressed urgently.

We also object to the wind farms in Cloggley, which may be visible from parts of the Royal Borough, and reserve the right to object to anything else that might affect us in a deleterious way. Otherwise we hope you will not bother us again.

Yours faithfully

J Sheene

Derek
I did warn you
about this one!!
Maybe we should have
a chat?   Barb.

Jeremy Sheene's letter on behalf of the Royal Borough of Dunromin

There was no reply from Golden Delicious.

GCC
grotton
county
council

Department of Transport and Environment
Donald MacDonald FICE MIMunE
PO Box 42
Grotton GR2 7DT

29 April 2006

Dear Derek

Re: Draft RSS

Thank you for your consultation on the draft RSS. It is most unfortunate that AGA has not been able to agree on a joint response; I know Mr Sheene has already apologised on behalf of the Leader of the Royal Borough of Dunromin who, though a man of the greatest integrity, is unfortunately prone to expressing his views in a particularly forthright way. We are hopeful of repairing the damage quickly however, and meanwhile we press on.

We note that several Districts express opposition to the number of houses you propose. The novel idea of building houses in Grimethwaite may be worth consideration in these circumstances, but of course the widespread pollution of air, land, and water renders this a shaky foundation (literally over much of the District) on which to base an entire strategy. We shall therefore argue for a re-evaluation of the approach to housing allocations, the better to reflect the realities on the ground.

This is particularly important from our point of view since, as the Transport Authority, it seems we are supposed to magic finance out of thin air in order to pay for the infrastructure needs which would ensue from your proposals. On its past record the Government will make no provision for this and S106 seems to be a dead duck. We note that at the present rate of financial assistance the list of entirely necessary transport schemes on pages 67–81 would not be completed until 3046.

We are grateful however to Grimethwaite for offering to accommodate the entire waste arisings in the County.

With thanks

Yours sincerely

Koffi Break

Koffi Break

The reply from the County Council

Mr Albatross from the GO had little option but to respond to the
Regional Assembly, eventually, in the following terms:

GOVERNMENT OFFICE FOR THE NORTH WEST

Incorporating MHLG, DOE, DETR, DTLR, ODPM, CLG, DfT, DECC,
whatever DBERR is called now, defra and possibly a few others

GROTTON REGIONAL OFFICE
DAN SMITH HOUSE, BACK SIDE STREET WEST, GROTTON GR11 9ZX

Ref: NW/GROT/AQ/GA/P60

10 August 2006

Derek

The Secretary of State wishes to see the housing allocations increased. As you know, she
has committed the Government to ensuring the construction of three million new homes
across the country within the next eighteen months or so and it is important that Grotton
provides its share. Almost any old houses will do so long as there are three million of
them, but we prefer them to be built at a very high density on brownfield land in order
to save building on green fields, which leads to a degree of unwelcome criticism of
Ministers.

Having said that, on the one hand, on the other hand etc. etc. (see previous letters on this
subject) …

Gerald Albatross.

Gerald Albatross
Authorised by the Minister to sign in that behalf

The Examination in Public was duly held some months later. Koffi Break represented the County, with all the others (including the City) disappointed to be watching only from the sidelines; when Jeremy Sheene asked why all the Districts could not take an active part in the proceedings, the reply he received was that if there was one thing worse in the Government's eyes than a democratic deficit, which as it happened it did not accept existed in this case, it was a democratic surplus.

There was much competition for the holding of the Examination, but the St Vitus United Primitive Evangelical Tabernacle and Community Hub in Cloggley was selected. Peter Rabbit knew it well as it was the location for his model railway society meetings; unfortunately he attended only at weekends and had failed to appreciate the impact of the children's nursery during the week. However the Wendy House was pressed into service as the Panel's retiring room, and the Programme Officer took up residence in the tree house in the old yew in the memorial garden. As the boxes of documents were trolleyed into the Examination, the children began crayoning on the Environmental Appraisal; the drawing of 'Daddy' on page 973 of Appendix 27C led to a somewhat fruitless debate on Day 19.

None of this was assisted by a public demonstration outside on the playground; shouts of 'What do we want?' – 'A Regional Spatial Strategy!' – 'When do we want it?' – '2016!' mingled with the screams of children traumatised by the sight of the CPRE's barrister emerging from the wigwam. Nonetheless, the Panel Chair, a man like all his colleagues of whom nothing has been heard since, pressed on and for seven weeks the future of the region was in the balance.

Koffi Break, renowned for his patience and persuasiveness, put the case for the County expertly (although it is not clear that anyone was listening). Representatives of the business community told the Panel that they wanted more transport links, more parking provision, more houses, schools and shops, more sites allocated for business in the Green Belt, fewer planners, and lower taxes. Representatives of environmental groups said more or less the opposite, except for the last bit.

The Panel arrived at a solution which was generally regarded as reasonable. But Ministers nevertheless increased the housing allocations across the board[2] – no surprise as they had done the same in every other region (providing continued employment for barristers and judges), even though the house building industry by this time had virtually ceased to be. Mr Quibble has since said that his office had of course anticipated the slump, but wanted the County to be in a good position to respond when the inevitable upturn arrived. At the take-up rate experienced in Grotton in around 2009, there were now 4500 years' worth of housing allocations – the highest in the developed world.

Local Development Frameworks

Alexander Quibble's letter, quoted earlier, went on to discuss local development frameworks (see opposite).

2 Subject to ongoing legal proceedings.

... I turn now, as you requested, to the question of Local Development Frameworks, which coincidentally I was discussing personally with the Minister recently. These were introduced after a lot of thought and any number of consultants' reports in 2004, as part of our modernisation of the planning system. They are essentially very simple. Your members may find the following summary helpful; if they ask you any difficult questions, I suggest you refer them to:

www.communities.gov.uk/planningandbuilding/planning/DevelopmentPlansforDummies

You should first produce a Local Development Scheme (LDS), which says what you are going to do. We have to agree to that, and you should of course be stretching yet realistic in your approach. You should produce a Statement of Community Involvement (SCI) which says how you will consult people, which you don't have to have an Inquiry into now though you used to, and then the Local Development Framework (LDF) itself. This is an evidence-based, front-loaded, outcome-focused portfolio of documents, shaped through a Sustainability Appraisal, and designed to be delivered through local partnerships. LDFs must include a Core Strategy (CS), a Site Specific Allocations document (SSA), and an Adopted Proposals Map (APM), which should be kept up to date. You may also prepare as many Area Action Plans (AAPs), Development Plan Documents (DPDs) and Supplementary Planning Documents (SPDs) as you wish, together with any Local Development Orders (LDOs) and Simplified Planning Zones (SPZs) you may require, though most people have forgotten about those. DPDs, SPDs, and the SCI are known collectively as Local Development Documents (LDDs). The CS, SSAs, APM, AAPs and other DPDs (together with the RSS) form the Development Plan itself, but the LDS, SCI, SPDs, LDOs and SPZs are not part of the Development Plan. You must also produce an Annual Monitoring Report (AMR), annually. And it goes without saying that all or most of these are subject to a Strategic Environmental Assessment (SEA), a Sustainability Appraisal (SA), an Appropriate Assessment (AA) under the Conservation (Natural Habitats &c) Regulations 1994 (the Habitats Regulations), a Health Impact Assessment (HIA), and an Equalities Impact Assessment (EIA).

There really isn't any more to it than that.

Sorry, yes there is.

You ask whether or not the dictum of 'survey, analysis, plan' is likely to come back into favour, on the grounds that the Government has abandoned the technique of 'predict and provide' and, more recently, 'plan, monitor and manage', and more recently still, 'love, honour and obey'. No such move has been mentioned in any of my many personal discussions with Ministers; my own view is that individual authorities should meld the best of these approaches, each of which has its undoubted merits, into an omnium gatherum which satisfies the demands of their own local circumstances.

You asked me to say a word about the tests of 'soundness'. Your plans must be justified, effective and consistent with national policy. This means of course that we can pretty well always find impurities and inexactitudes should the need arise.

I hope your colleagues in the AGA will accept that the modernised system which the Government has put in place is in fact entirely sensible, and the best advice I can offer you is to move ahead with all possible speed.

Yours ever

Alexander Quibble

Alexander Quibble

III

This, of course, was of immeasurable help and the Districts are now moving ahead, though not in every case with all possible speed. There was however a twist in the tail when a Freedom of Information Act enquiry revealed that Mr Quibble, confused by his own circumlocution, had asked one of his colleagues in Eland House (recently arrived from his old college) to consider whether there might be any alternative, simpler system. The astonishing suggestion he received was that there should be just one single plan for each Authority, covering absolutely everything. What could be more straightforward than that? It would cover all aspects of growth and regeneration throughout the whole of each District, allocate land for various uses, set out every change proposed, define the Green Belt, protect the environment, sort out transport, and generally do the whole job in one document.

Quibble took informal soundings on this idea from stakeholders, and was surprised by the response. The President of the RTPI, for example, sent an e-mail on the following lines:

From: rsj@rtpi.org
To: a.quibble51@gonw.gsi.gov.uk
Sent: 25 April 2008 19.44
Subject: Not again!

>> You blithering idiot. We've tried that. It doesn't work. Everyone hated it. Takes too long. Somebody objects to something and the whole bloody thing gets held up. Then you grumble about my members as usual. You seem to think you can just muck around with the rules every five minutes, keep issuing stonking great reports that nobody has time to download, patronise us from atop your prodigious mountains of elephantine ignorance, then say it's all our fault. Get a grip. Sorry – did I leave my tablets in your office?

Mediating space, making place!

RSJ

Quite understandably, no more has been heard of this idea.

So How are the Authorities Getting on with their LDFs?

At the time of writing, the honest answer to this question is 'fair to middling'.

The full details of where the Grotton Councils are up to can, of course, be found by accessing their various websites, where a considerable amount of out-of-date information is freely available, but the particular examples of Cloggley and Dunromin may provide a useful basis for a 'case study' (this is of course necessary in an academic book such as the one you have been kind enough to purchase).

Cloggley

Cloggley, as indicated earlier, is having to accommodate large amounts of housing and thus has a programme to prepare several plans for its growth areas. They are finding this a challenge. They ran into particular trouble over the expansion of Upper Gumtry, and Peter Rabbit found it necessary to write to Alexander Quibble:

Affordable housing in Cloggley has not always been of the highest quality

Cloggley District Council

Planning and Public Health Section
P. Rabbit
Borough Planning and Estates Officer (temp) (ret'd)
Elsie Street
Cloggley GR47 8QZ

1 October 2008

Dear Alexander

I'm sorry to bother you with the problems of Cloggley since I am sure you have a great deal on your plate. We have not in fact met since you arrived from whichever Department it was. Though I have attended a number of meetings of various Committees of which you are a member you have always (quite understandably) been too busy to attend yourself. Generally speaking you have sent your Mr Albatross along. I would just like to say how pleased I am that he is doing so well at the GO. As you know he used to work here and he is in fact the only person I have ever had to discipline for laziness and incompetence. I understand that he had similarly failed to realise his potential at Grotton City Council, and that subsequently he performed disappointingly at Dunromin. How good it is to see you giving a chance to Mr Albatross and I am sure it gives you pride to see him representing HM Government in this way after such an unpromising start to his career.

Unfortunately, however, the guidance he has given at the Regional Co-ordinating Committee number 18 on Development Plans has been slightly unclear, hence the need to trouble you in this way. As you know, the Regional Strategy requires Cloggley to provide for 2500 houses, as a contribution to the Government's target. We are of course anxious to help in this regard, even though getting even one house built in the present climate is proving difficult. Messrs Bettabuild, the biggest firm in the County, after firing almost all of their staff, have now resorted to selling off their private helicopter. I think this demonstrates the scale of the problem.

We have had a go at producing a Core Strategy. This is apparently a requirement, so we are well on the way. And we have also made a start on a Local Development Document (or it may be an Action Area Plan or a Supplementary Planning Document – could you please tell us which would be best?) for the rather daunting expansion of Upper Gumtry. The snag is that most of the residents are likely to be unhappy at this prospect and prefer that development goes instead to Upton-on-t'Bogg, though the potential for flooding there is well recognised as the Bogg overflows at regular intervals due to inadequate maintenance upstream.

There's also the point that Upper Gumtry itself has already been subject to rapid growth in recent years, don't you think? Jemima says that a nice little village has turned into a mere dormitory settlement for Grotton, which isn't very 'sustainable'; she has certainly picked up some of the technical jargon from me over the years! And the traffic going past our house every morning is getting worse all the time. We almost lost Oedipuss under a lorry the other morning.

Anyway, sorry to ramble, but if it isn't too much trouble I just wondered if you had any thoughts on this difficult problem. After all it is you who wants us to build all these houses!!!!

Yours ever

Peter Rabbit
Borough Planning and Estates Officer

PS I think I read in 'Planning' about something called an eco-town. I wonder if we ought to have one of those? Perhaps you could explain what it is since no one I have spoken to has the slightest idea and your Mr Albatross simply looked embarrassed when I mentioned it.

Mr Quibble replied only three months later:

GOVERNMENT OFFICE FOR THE NORTH WEST

Incorporating MHLG, DOE, DETR, DTLR, ODPM, CLG, DfT, DECC,
whatever DBERR is called now, defra and possibly a few others

GROTTON REGIONAL OFFICE
DAN SMITH HOUSE, BACK SIDE STREET WEST, GROTTON GR11 9ZX

Ref: NW/GROT/AQ/P60
12 January 2009

The obvious need for more housing in Cloggley

Dear Mr Rabid

Thank you very much indeed for your most interesting letter of … It is most unfortunate that we have not yet met but you obviously appreciate the many calls on my time which make it more difficult than I would like to attend to matters such as planning which are of course so very important to the future of the region and indeed the nation in these troubled times and to which it is incumbent upon all of us to pay the closest attention, unless of course there are other calls on one's time, as there so often are in these challenging times, and this is particularly so in my own case due to the very wide range of responsibilities carried by my office all of which demand my closest attention, for example the problems of quite large and important places like Manchester and to some extent Liverpool which inevitably somewhat overshadow Cloggthorpe, and the current temporary economic difficulties through which the nation is going as a result of global forces and not in any way as a result of anything this or any other British Government might have done.

I am pleased you appreciate the need to build three million houses – not all of them in Cleggley of course!! The Government's projections, taking into account household growth, migration, and a range of other complex and sophisticated assumptions which you really need not bother with, clearly show that this requirement exists. It is also quite clear that the planning system has stood in the way of achieving this target. House builders have consistently told us that this is so, and it is essential to respond to this positively. It is clearly as a direct result of the planning system that the price of housing has risen so much. I am pleased to see that Clogglea agrees with this view. I am sure the problems of Messrs Bettabuild are temporary and that soon they will go back to complaining about the planners just as they did in the olden days.

As to the difficulties you anticipate with some of your residents, it is of course not a matter for me to tell you how to plan your Borough. You have complete freedom to plan the area as your democratically elected Council wishes, though of course you must provide for 2500 houses and you won't get any money from us unless you do.

If you have any further problems please contact Mr Albatross. I hope this is helpful.

Yours sincerely

Alexander Quibble

Alexander Quibble

PS You mention eco-towns. On the whole I think it would be best if you didn't.

Cloggley went ahead with the preparation of both the Core Strategy and the Upper Gumtry and District Area Planning Strategy and Handy Road Atlas. They followed all the guidance faithfully, noting for example that a 'sustainability appraisal' was required by S19(5) of the Act and taking careful steps to find out exactly what that was.

Cloggley's Statement of Community Involvement had raised a certain frisson of excitement in the planning world when first published. Peter Rabbit proposed to visit every resident of the Borough for a nice cup of tea and a chance to think things through. Fortunately – this having proved beyond his powers

of time management – various fall-backs had been included. Not only was a fish supper held at St Vitus's for working class consultees, but a stand was taken at the bring and buy sale at the old folks' home, and a letter was pushed personally by Mr Rabbit through every letter box in Upper Gumtry.

Naturally this led to a number of representations. However Cloggley are proceeding with the plan and the appointed Inspector Ms B M W Campbell is due to take up occupation of the Wendy House shortly and consider the points raised. A lengthy Examination is anticipated.

<u>This is not a Circular</u>

Dear friend

Town and Country Planning Act 2004

This is Peter Rabbit, your planning chap, here. We've had to prepare a bit of a plan for Upper Gumtry, and I'm sort of responsible for it. Of course you may have heard already from the Upper Gumtry Heritage Group (UGH), who are telling us they think we've got it a bit wrong, and I can see their point. It is true as they say that we are intending that some houses will be built in the village. There are a considerable number of houses already there, as you know, as this letter is being put through your letter box, so you must already live in one of them, but now there will be some more. Well, quite a lot actually.

Now I don't want to try to blame someone else for all this. But the fact is that Mr Quibble of the Government Office has told us to provide these houses. Apparently there is a shortage. We've been given a lot of figures about this, which you are welcome to have a look at, though I'm finding it hard to follow myself, but anyway I hope you understand that we're just doing our best. If you want to tell us that you object to all these houses, that's quite OK and we won't be hurt. But I hope you won't be too unpleasant about it if we meet in the Co-op, as it's all a bit of a strain and Mrs Rabbit is saying I must take it easy.

Toodle Pip

Peter

The personal letter from Peter Rabbit

Dunromin

The punctilious meticulousness with which Dunromin have ensured that every stage of the planning process is followed to the letter, often several times, is admired by students of best practice the world over.

The Statement of Community Involvement provides an illustration of this, being utterly comprehensive, and subject in itself to elaborate community involvement via an innovative process known as 'quadruple deliberation'; it also includes the telephone directory as an appendix. To help them in this task, the Council employed a range of marketing consultants and PR experts, all of whom – for a surprising fee – could guarantee to continue consultation processes for as long as the Council wished.

Inevitably, this commitment to excellence meant that both the Core Strategy and the Grotton Gateway Area Action Plan (which dealt with the main area of proposed development in the Royal Borough) were somewhat delayed. There had been some damaging accusations along the way, following the leaking of a briefing note from Jeremy Sheene to the Council Leader which referred to the new process as 'offering unlimited potential for creating the illusion of speed via the complexity of constant equivocation', and the opportunity it presented 'for taking the fullest advantage of the manifold possibilities for obfuscation afforded by the accidental and deliberate intricacy of the Government's sundry and shifting pronouncements and prescriptions'.

An example of Dunromin's comprehensive approach is the questionnaire sent out to a random sample of 50% of the inhabitants by consultants Askham and Probe, of Mayfair (see opposite).

Dunromin Local Development Framework Core Strategy:

Your chance to influence **our** plans!

The Royal Borough of Dunromin has to prepare a Core Strategy. The purpose of this is to replace the Local Plan under the old planning system, with which you will be familiar as we consulted you on it several times. We never quite managed to complete that plan of course, but this proved no problem since what you told us consistently during those consultations was that you really didn't want a plan, or at least not one that contained any proposals. We took that to heart and this proves our commitment to listening to your views.

What is a Core Strategy anyway?

Well it's a bit complicated. But in plain language it's a big plan which says what's going to happen over the next very long time. Well, not really a *plan* as such – more a collection of words and phrases which we call *policies*. There will be a sort of plan to go with it of course – well, more a kind of a diagram.

How will it help?

It will help us to build a better Dunromin (or alternatively to leave it exactly as it is). It will safeguard our children's future. It will make life worth living again.

Will it affect my house?

Well the thing is it's very hard to tell at this stage. And even if we knew (and as it happens we've a pretty shrewd idea), we're not allowed to tell you in this plan. What you need is an "action area" plan, and we may get round to doing one of those if we ever finish this one.

How much will it cost?

Not as much as you might think

Why has it taken so long?

Look, to start with some people have taken a lot longer than us and anyway as we've said we seem to have managed perfectly well without one all this time so why all the fuss? As it happens it's a very difficult job planning a whole Royal Borough and it doesn't make it any easier if people keep criticising us.

What am I supposed to do about it?

It's your future and your Dunromin. So your views are what we want. Fill in the simple questionnaire (form) and put it out with the recycling. It will be collected in a few days. Then sit back and relax and leave the rest to us.

Issued by the Royal Borough of Dunromin in the interests of public convenience.

DUNROMIN: YOUR TOWN – HAVE YOUR SAY!

Question 1   Name and address (if known)..

Question 2   Age (circle all appropriate)   1-5   5-60   60-65   65-120   Other

Question 3   Sex   a in the garden   b at the theatre   c in bed
                         d under the car   e with friends
If b, how long does it usually take to get there?

Question 4   In your leisure time do you like to be   a male   b female   c other
Question 5   What would you miss most if we knocked your house down?

Question 6   Given the choice, which of the following alternatives would you prefer?
                    a a lovely new park with a swimming pool and a floral clock
                    b a festering smelly tip at the bottom of the garden

                    a a nice wide road and a free car parking space at the other end
                    b a bus
If you choose b please give reasons

Question 7   Where 1 equals total agreement and 5 equals total disgust, indicate how much you
agree with the following statements:

The countryside doesn't really matter - it's just a load of fields and things	1	2	3	4	5
New housing estates really improve the environment and we should have a lot more of them especially near where I live	1	2	3	4	5
Dunromin needs a lot more working class people to balance it up a bit	1	2	3	4	5
Thank God for the planners who are stopping Dunromin from being concreted over	1	2	3	4	5
Post Offices are a waste of time anyway	1	2	3	4	5

Question 8   Are there any other useful observations or ideas which you feel you would like to make in order to assist the Royal Borough in preparing this really important plan? I think the plan.........

Question 9   Do you think that planners are an honest hard-working underpaid bunch of people who are only trying to do their best in difficult circumstances?   Yes

Next use your skill and judgement to answer this simple question:
Do you like Dunromin just as it is now?   Yes   No
(A £20 Harvey Nichols voucher will be given for each correct answer)

Now complete the following sentence in not more than 12 (that's twelve) of your own words:
I don't mind if the Core Strategy is never finished because............ ....

[Please note that owing to a pritning error the answers to Q3 should be selected from the options in Q 4 and vice versa]

It became clear from this and other surveys that 100% (plus or minus 5) of the population preferred Dunromin as it was about twenty years ago, whenever that was. This was further demonstrated in letters and e-mails to the local paper, the following being just two examples:

Letters to the Editor

Sir
So the Government has decided to inflict yet more development on the lovely and historic District of Dunromin. I have lived here man and boy since 1897. I am a man of the world – I saw action in the Crimean War and travelled as far as Llandudno on caravan trips with my late wife. I don't mind change. Only last week I got a man to move my sideboard from under the window to just behind the door to the conservatory. But this Government which is full of lefties and demagogues now says that just because there are homeless people they are going to build houses somewhere near here, destroying all I have stood for, whatever it is, and ruining the environment for future generations, even though most of them are a lot of useless layabouts.

Until my house was built here in 1991 this was a beautiful place and I want it to remain so for the sake of my grandchildren, though sadly owing to Mrs Harbringer-Grudge's deficiency in the hormone department we never had children, but the principle stands. Get this appalling Government out at once! What they are doing is finishing off what the Luftwaffe started, but this Government is worse than that, apart from all the killing of course, and they will destroy this town as sure as I live and breathe, which is not much these days but I still have the right to a point of view and I know I represent the views of the people of this conspicuous town, why won't they listen, it's a disgrace, whatever it is, and should be stopped.
Lt Col R J H Harbringer-Grudge (ret'd)
'Upanattem', Wobberleigh

None of this came as a surprise to Jeremy Sheene, and as part of his carefully designed programme of taking action without doing anything, he wrote pointlessly to Mr Quibble (writing to Mr Quibble was always pointless) along the following lines:

Royal Borough of
Dunromin

Office of the Chief Executive
JEREMY SHEENE MBE MA (Oxon) FRICS FIBA FIMS ACCA
Civic Centre, Prince Regent Square
Bletherley GR9 5AY

29 Feb 2008

Speeding up the Local Development Framework

Dear Mr Quibble

We have of course been working with the greatest degree of commitment and earnestness towards meeting the targets set for us, quite unreasonably in our view, by your office through the "Regional Spatial Strategy". As you know this is still the subject of legal action in the Courts, and I shall be in Strasbourg talking to our lawyers next week. However, your Department made it clear that unless we made progress there could be unspecified financial consequences for the Royal Borough. We have therefore, under protest and with the greatest degree of reluctance, set in train a transparent and thorough process leading to the preparation of a plan for the Grotton Gateway – the area of Dunromin which was allocated for expansion in the Town Map of 1966, the Structure Plan of 1984, and the District wide Local Plan of 1997, but which as yet we have been unable to find a way of developing in a way which is satisfactory to my Members.

We have as you know (because I am aware that you are a resident of one of the more select parts of Bletherley) carried out one of the most thorough public consultation processes ever devised. The results of this have been clear. Approximately one hundred percent of the residents of the Royal Borough are opposed to any development at all in the Grotton Gateway area (which they prefer to describe as the Cramshaw Superior Country Park designate). In the light of this, we propose to reduce the proposed number of new dwellings from 1200 to 43, which we feel can be sensitively laid out in the form of an attractive micro-eco-town around a small lake in such a way as to retain the essential character of the area whilst attracting the sort of people (such as yourself) who appreciate the qualities of the Royal Borough and who would enhance its economy and its property values. My members hope you will agree that this goes a reasonable way towards meeting your targets.

Your Mr Albatross was unable to give us a clear view on this important matter, though he did mutter something about your Department having the power to intervene in some unspecified way. This, it seems to my Members, would be to negate the democratic process, and I am sure you would not contemplate such a step. It is however a matter I shall be discussing informally with my friend Mr Charles Silke QC,[3] who is always most helpful in these matters.

Yours sincerely

Jeremy Sheene MBE
Chief Executive

---

3 When asked, in relation to a controversial case in which he was involved, 'What did you add to that public Inquiry?', Mr Silke replied 'about two and a half years' – Ed.

And the reply came winging back, in due course:

GOVERNMENT OFFICE FOR THE NORTH WEST

Incorporating MHLG, DOE, DETR, DTLR, ODPM, CLG, DfT, DECC,
whatever DBERR is called now, defra and possibly a few others

GROTTON REGIONAL OFFICE
DAN SMITH HOUSE, BACK SIDE STREET WEST, GROTTON GR11 9ZX

Ref: NW/GROT/AQ/P60
12 December 2009

The possible need for new housing in Dunromin

Dear Mr Sheene

Thank you for your recent letter. I must apologise for the delay in replying but as I am sure you appreciate there are many calls on my time … (reproduce the 1st para of the letter to Peter Rabbi).

I must of course put on one side my own interest in this matter as a resident of Cramshaw Superior. It would be quite improper of me to comment, beyond noting that it is indeed a most attractive area and that the development of the Grotton Gateway would have a damaging effect on the environment and indeed on house prices, such as they are. I will not allow myself to be influenced by such matters.

I think it best that you proceed with your revised plan, and place it before one of Her Majesty's Inspectors in due course. Mr Albatross is right in that we do have powers to intervene in these matters and to take over the preparation of the Plan ourselves. However this is a power which has been very rarely (indeed never) used, and I think you can rest reasonably assured that I shall not be recommending Ministers take such a course of action in respect of a well-run Authority such as the Royal Borough.

If you have any further questions please contact Mr Albatross.

Yours sincerely

Alexander Quibble

Alexander Quibble

Following this exchange, and against Sheene's better judgement, some progress was for a time made in Dunromin. Unfortunately this was not in a forward direction, and Inspector Ms B M W Campbell had to wait nearly a year for the opportunity to hold a public examination in Bletherley, where the sandwiches at lunchtime come from Marks and Spencer, usually followed by a scrumptious dessert of fruit, jelly and cream. But this is a mere trifle. Sheene's ruthless and indefatigable approach to the topic (which is in contrast to the somewhat ruth and defatigable approach of other Districts) has continued the Dunromin tradition, established in the 1960s, of fending off development in the Cramshaw Superior area, whatever the Government and whatever the statistical imperatives.

At the time of writing, the plan has just failed all the tests of soundness and has been returned to Dunromin for a fresh start to be made. Quietly satisfied, Mr Sheene has gone on an extended holiday to the Galapagos.

The position with the other authorities can briefly be summarised:

Grotton City Council prefer the flexibility of not having plans at all but see the need to prepare them, if only in order to get their hands on the grants that go with them. With this in mind, they have made considerable progress on an expansionist Core Strategy which they describe as 'pliable and open-ended'. Following criticism by the Inspector, Ms Campbell, they now accept that whilst a flexible approach is desirable, it will in fact now be necessary to prepare some policies to go with it.

Grimethwaite's extant Local Plan was formally adopted in 1997. In its draft form it contained only one policy – one which reflected the generous and open-minded attitude to development adopted by the District:

GEN1

Any application for planning permission will be approved

Reasoned justification

Things could hardly get any worse

The then Department of the Environment were unhappy with this policy, which they considered to be insufficiently flexible. Following a lengthy report from the Inspector, the policy was changed to read:

GEN1

Pretty much any application for planning permission will be approved

This policy served Grimethwaite well enough, given the largely complete absence of any applications to deal with, but of course the soundness tests which apply to the new planning system are rather fierce and Grimethwaite realised that they would not be able to get away with anything so vague and open to interpretation now. As a result, the revised version reads:

GEN1

Every application will be approved on its merits

Reasoned justification

Things have in fact got worse

The report of the Inspector at the Examination into that plan is one of the shorter ones. It reads, in full:

'As there were understandably no objections to this policy, which seems to me to encapsulate a subtle balance of certainty, flexibility and pointlessness, I hereby recommend that the Plan is adopted forthwith and I very much hope things get better soon. Love and Best Wishes, B M W Campbell (Ms).'

Golden Delicious – reports awaited.

Grotton County Council are well advanced with their new Minerals and Waste Development Document,[4] possibly because they have little else to do, and anyway nobody can stop them. They have already completed a Hard Core Strategy,[5] which is remarkably boring.

4 This is completely different from a Minerals and Waste Local Plan of course (enquiries to the County Council please).

5 Readers googling this phrase are advised to be careful.

Grimethwaite's stunning new 'Retail Outlet Mall' is ready for business

Conclusion

It seems that the Grotton authorities are making a rather better fist of preparing plans under the new system than many others. 'Success' being an unfamiliar concept in the Grotton context, it may be best to put this down to the quite breathtaking failure of authorities elsewhere to grasp the opportunities offered by the new(ish) system, whatever they are.

Bletherley Borough Planning Committee enjoy a well-earned break circa 1962

chapter four

Development Management in Crisis
A Case Study from Dunromin

The Scene

It is nine o'clock on a wet Wednesday morning in Prince Regent Square, Bletherley. Mr Horace Belcher, now retired from the old family firm of Belchers the Butchers ('The Land of Lard'), has made his arthritic way up the Civic Centre[1] steps, past the imposing equestrian statue of Lord Kitchener (who did very little for the town) and through the revolving door (twice). He pauses for breath and looks about him. Things have changed a lot since he was last here. Instead of the bland anonymity which he still remembers from his previous visit (some time in 1973, when he popped in to pay his gas and water rates), he finds himself entering a bright and cheerful space, generously provided with overstuffed sofas and rows of certificates from the Investors in People people, and generally humming with quiet efficiency …

He is immediately greeted with a huge illuminated sign reading:

> **DUNROMIN BOROUGH COUNCIL
> CENTRAL CUSTOMER–FOCUS
> ARRIVALS, TRIAGE AND DESPATCH CAPABILITY**

Impressed, he follows a flashing arrow which hangs beneath the sign, passes unawares through the Facial Cognitive Biometric Queue Management System, which electronically tags him with the number 112 (while probably noting his credit card details) and considers the series of eye-catching options which then present themselves on an illuminated display.

The first of these signs reads:

> **FOR *SERIOUS* COMPLAINTS ONLY:
> ALL DEPARTMENTS EXCEPT PLANNING**

the next:

> **PLANNING COMPLAINTS (<u>ALL</u>)**

and the third:

> **ALL OTHER ENQUIRIES**

Mr Belcher has no complaints about the planners, at least not yet, so he simply decides to sink into one of the sofas, peruse his *Racing Times*, and await the arrival of his agent. But he can't relax – after all, this is his big day: in just under an hour, the men and women of the Development Management and Continuous Performance Improvement Panel (which he thinks used to be called the Planning Committee) will sit in judgement, for the second time, on the project he has been dreaming about day and night for the last eighteen months.

---

1 Crabtree, Evelyn and Seifert, 1971 (described by Pevsner N *et al.* in *Forgotten Civic Centres of England*).

The air-conditioning system wafts essence of skinny latte and chives around the room, while strains of *Sheep May Safely Graze* are heard from some discreetly hidden loudspeakers. It is a sheer delight to be here. The atmosphere is so soporific, in fact, that Mr Belcher is on the point of dozing off, when he is suddenly woken by a cheery *Bing Bong* over the public address system:

> 'Good morning and welcome to visitors who have just joined us. This is Damien, your Customer Management Services Manager. On behalf of the whole of the team here at Dunromin Council, I hope you are having a pleasant and relaxing wait while your complaint is being registered ...'

And now here, somewhat dishevelled and sweating with the effort of lugging around a complete set of the *Encyclopaedia of Planning Law*, is Gerry Pottle, Consultant Town Planner, looking older than his 51 years would suggest, but still managing to exude an amiable (if not quite convincing) air of boundless optimism. He greets his client, checks his watch and ushers Mr Belcher towards the Council Chamber he knows so well …

But First, the Story so Far …

The story begins nearly two years earlier.

Mr Belcher's uncle had left him the title deeds to what was left of Lugg Farm, a run-down plot of land, extending to about half an acre in old money, containing a semi-derelict farmhouse, and a characterful group of middens, byres and similar local terms, in the Green Belt about half a mile outside the picturebook village of Cramshaw Superior.

Despite its unpromising appearance, Mr Belcher had convinced himself that his inheritance represented a once-in-a-lifetime development opportunity. Surely building a house at Cramshaw Fold could be his way of avoiding the pensions melt-down, the urban riots and the rising sea levels which everyone else seemed to be worried about? Maybe it would suit one of the dashing young footballers who were so much in evidence these days? In the event, however, his decision was made for him: Mrs Belcher had long craved a residence in Cramshaw, and had already acquired the John Lewis credit card that would be needed to furnish it to the appropriate standard. A retirement home it would be.

Mr Belcher was not completely daft. While his aspirations remained undimmed, he knew that there was a planning system, and that its writ almost certainly ran to include Cramshaw Superior. He needed to find out more.

According to his local telephone directory, information about all the Council's services was to be found by simply dialing 0845 000 444. After twenty minutes, during which time he had patiently selected option 4, followed by option 2, followed by option 8, followed by the hash key, followed by making a mistake and starting again, he finally reached planning inquiries. Only then was he rewarded with a recorded message which explained that the person he needed to speak to was either on holiday, at lunch, or on drugs.

He soon realized that his first port of call should, of course, have been the Council's website, although this was not a feature of life with which he was as yet overfamiliar. Having first sought the advice of his three-year-old grandson on how to switch on his computer, he settled down in his study with a large brandy, and began to interrogate his search engine. He soon realized that he didn't need to shout in order to do this, but progress was slow nevertheless. Eventually (having been diverted on the way by some interesting guidance on how to apply for a lap-dancing licence and what to do in an air raid) he was finally rewarded with something called *'Dunromin's Home-from-Home page'*.

Given the impressive range of helpful information it contained, it wasn't immediately clear to Mr Belcher which of the various links he should follow, but as luck would have it, he soon stumbled upon a most useful-looking box headed: *Thinking About Making a Planning Application?* This is what he found when he got there:

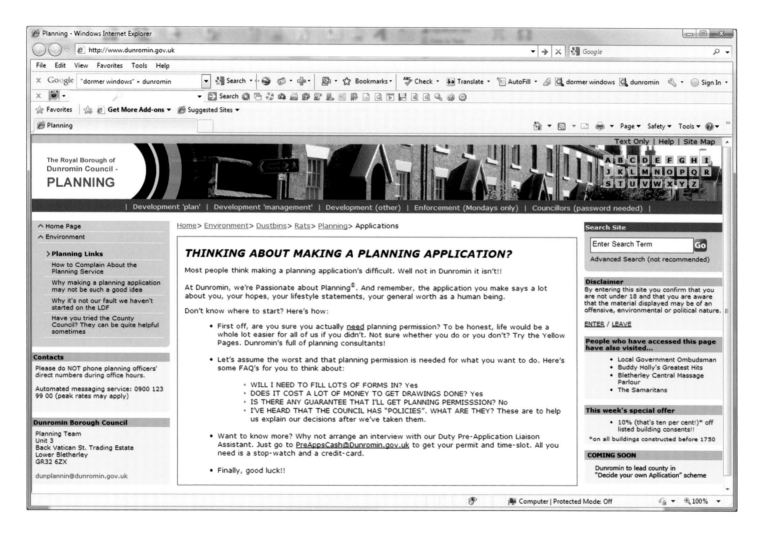

This advice had the desired effect – it put Mr Belcher off the whole idea.

Some weeks later, he was walking past what used to be a branch of the Bletherley Building Society (since absorbed into the Kazakhstan Sovereign Funds Investment Entity) when he found his way blocked by a smart-looking individual with a suspicious-looking tan and a toothy grin who, before he knew it, had thrust into his hands a brightly coloured leaflet headed TROUBLE WITH THE PLANNERS? PASS IT TO THE POTTLES! before disappearing into the crowds. Mr Belcher thought no more about the incident; but when he got home, he fished the leaflet out of his pocket, and this is what he read:

TROUBLE WITH THE PLANNERS?

PASS IT TO THE POTTLES!

Why bring your planning problems to Pottle and Wife? Well for starters, Gerry Pottle has an unrivalled experience of the planning system, having been around since the creation of the Bletherley District-wide Local Plan of 1988, which he helped to fold up. So he knows what stuff like this means:

"Proposals falling within categories a) to f) of Policy ENV5 (as saved) will normally (subject to the exceptions set out in Policy ECON1) be acceptable in principle, but only insofar as they would

(1) not give rise to inappropriate levels of disamenity for the occupiers of neighbouring residential heriditaments

(2) avoid contributing negatively to the sustainable regeneration of the Priority Areas, as set out in criteria (ii) to (xiii) of Policy STRAT2 (as proposed to be modified) and

(3) comply with other relevant polices of the Local Plan."

Let's face it, planning's not for the faint-hearted! But if you know which buttons to bend and which ears to push, you're half-way there. And that's where Pottles come in.

All enquiries treated in the strictest confidence.

And here's the best bit: **NO WIN, NO FEE!** In other words, if we don't get planning permission for something* at the end of the day, you don't pay a penny!!

*not necessarily what you applied for. Terms and conditions apply. E and O E. Subject to eligibility and status. Personal callers by appointment only. No connection with any other business of a similar nature / name / newspaper article.

Two days later, an excited Mr Belcher was in Pottle's smart office in downtown Bletherley (above what used to be *Spanish Properties 'R' Us*) describing his modest aspirations for Lugg Farm.

And what he heard delighted him: 'Leave it to me,' he had been told; 'I used to share a desk with the bloke who wrote the Local Plan policies for Dunromin – know them like the back of my hand!' (Pottle did not go into any details as to why he was no longer employed by the Authority, beyond hinting darkly that the Leader of the Council had suggested he spend more time with his family.)

He listened carefully to his new client's ideas: Mr Belcher didn't want to be greedy – surely the planners couldn't object to a nice little bungalow on the site of the old farmhouse, perhaps with some shrubs? 'Well it's not quite as simple as that,' said Pottle. 'It's in the Green Belt, you see, so they won't like it *in principle* – not an expression I've much time for myself, but there it is. We've got to box clever on this one. But don't worry, I've been there, got the tee-shirt, know the ropes. Where there's a will etc., etc.!'

Belcher hired him on the spot.

After seeing his latest prospect off the premises, and pausing only to double his hourly rate, Pottle's first move was to get in touch with his old friend Damien Hawkes-Blather RIBA. While his best days were, perhaps, behind him, Damien could still be relied upon to knock up an impressive perspective or two, obscure unhelpful details with generous landscaping and generally look on the bright side of an unpromising project; and once introduced to the Cramshaw job, he did not disappoint. After a liquid lunch with Pottle, he spent ten minutes or so producing an impressive set of sketches (remarkably, he saw no need to visit the site in order to do this – probably because the scheme bore a striking resemblance to several others that he had devised for different clients over the years), and had taken a break before preparing his invoice.

Pottle had then arranged to visit the planning department to size up the opposition, which, despite his optimistic assessment for the benefit of his client, he did not underestimate. The file note of his meeting with Polly Bingley, a graduate planner on a short-term contract from Australia, is reproduced below:

Pottle had, of course, anticipated this lukewarm response from Dunromin's planners, which is why he had instructed Hawkes-Blather to prepare *two* schemes. He knew perfectly well that the first would be dismissed out of hand; but this would enable him to describe the second as a 'compromise' designed to sit more comfortably within the Council's policy framework (or, at least, his interpretation of it). The revised proposal, significantly scaled down from the earlier version, is shown on the following pages and, without any further discussion with Ms Bingley, this formed the basis of Mr Belcher's planning application.

In addition, to help the Council fully understand his approach to the project, Mr Hawkes-Blather produced a document to accompany the application (see page 64).

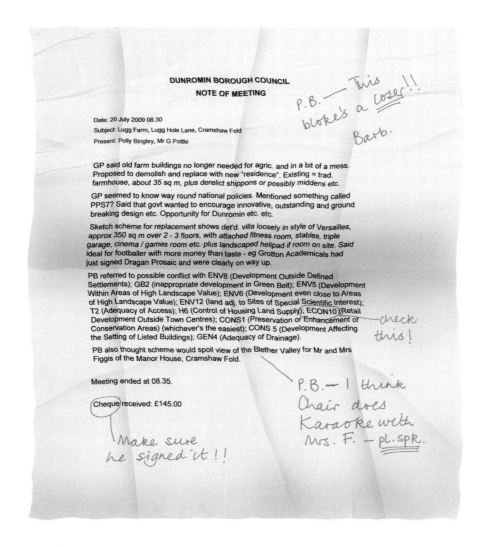

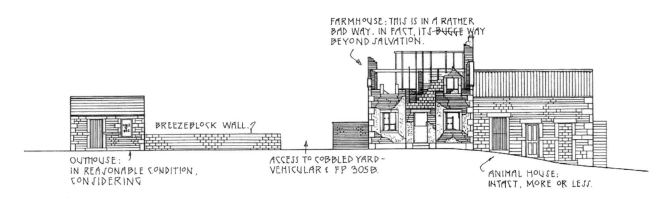

FARMHOUSE: THIS IS IN A RATHER
BAD WAY. IN FACT, IT'S ~~BUGGE~~ WAY
BEYOND SALVATION.

BREEZEBLOCK WALL.?

OUTHOUSE:
IN REASONABLE CONDITION,
CONSIDERING

ACCESS TO COBBLED YARD -
VEHICULAR & FP 305B.

ANIMAL HOUSE:
INTACT, MORE OR LESS.

ELEVATION FROM LUGG HOLE LANE

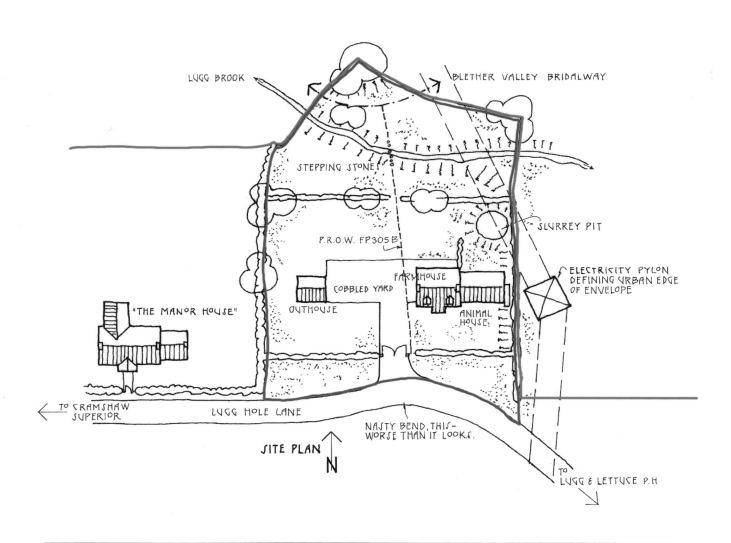

LUGG BROOK

BLETHER VALLEY BRIDALWAY

STEPPING STONE!

P.R.O.W. FP 305 B

SLURREY PIT

ELECTRICITY PYLON
DEFINING URBAN EDGE
OF ENVELOPE

FARMHOUSE

COBBLED YARD

"THE MANOR HOUSE"

OUTHOUSE

ANIMAL
HOUSE:

TO CRAMSHAW
SUPERIOR

LUGG HOLE LANE

NASTY BEND, THIS -
WORSE THAN IT LOOKS.

SITE PLAN
N

TO
LUGG & LETTUCE P.H

SURVEY OF EXISTING: LUGG FARM: LUGG HOLE LANE, CRAMSHAW FOLD

CAREFULLY MEASURED and ACCURATELY DRAWN UP

SCALE: PROBABLY NOT TO SCALE

DRAWING NO: 009DH-B 01

BY: DAHABLA DESIGN
C O N S U L T A N T S

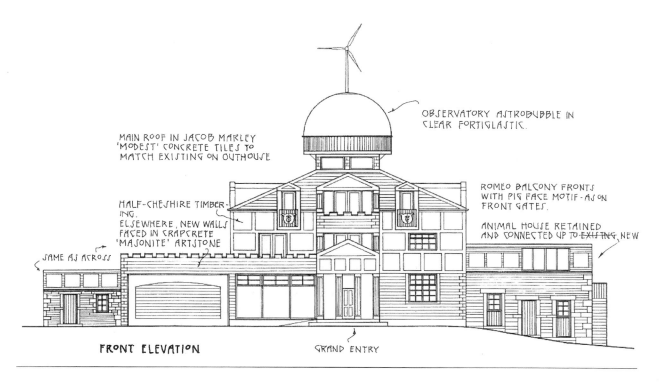

OBSERVATORY ASTROBUBBLE IN CLEAR FORTIGLASTIC.

MAIN ROOF IN JACOB MARLEY 'MODEST' CONCRETE TILES TO MATCH EXISTING ON OUTHOUSE

HALF-CHESHIRE TIMBER-ING. ELSEWHERE, NEW WALLS FACED IN CRAPCRETE 'MASONITE' ARTSTONE

SAME AS ACROSS

ROMEO BALCONY FRONTS WITH PIG FACE MOTIF - AS ON FRONT GATES.

ANIMAL HOUSE RETAINED AND CONNECTED UP TO EXISTING NEW

FRONT ELEVATION

GRAND ENTRY

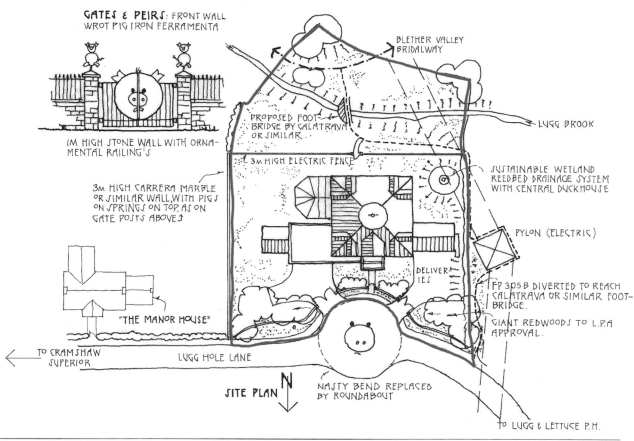

GATES & PEIRS: FRONT WALL WROT PIG IRON FERRAMENTA

1M HIGH STONE WALL WITH ORNA-MENTAL RAILING'S

3M HIGH CARRERA MARBLE OR SIMILAR WALL, WITH PIGS ON SPRINGS ON TOP, AS ON GATE POSTS ABOVES

"THE MANOR HOUSE"

TO CRAMSHAW SUPERIOR

LUGG HOLE LANE

BLETHER VALLEY BRIDALWAY

PROPOSED FOOT-BRIDGE BY CALATRAVA OR SIMILAR.

3M HIGH ELECTRIC FENCE

LUGG BROOK

SUSTAINABLE WETLAND REEDBED DRAINAGE SYSTEM WITH CENTRAL DUCKHOUSE

PYLON (ELECTRIC)

DELIVER-IES

FP 305 B DIVERTED TO REACH CALATRAVA OR SIMILAR FOOT-BRIDGE.

GIANT REDWOODS TO L.P.A APPROVAL.

SITE PLAN N

NASTY BEND REPLACED BY ROUNDABOUT

TO LUGG & LETTUCE P.H.

PROPOSED:	"PIG'S EAR"- NEW DWELLING REPLACING LUGG FARMHOUSE LUGG HOLE LANE, CRAMSHAW FOLD
CREATED FOR:	MR. & MRS. HORACE BELCHER
SCALE:	(ALL DIFFERENT)

DRAWING NO: 009DH-B 02

BY:

DAHABLA DESIGN
C O N S U L T A N T S

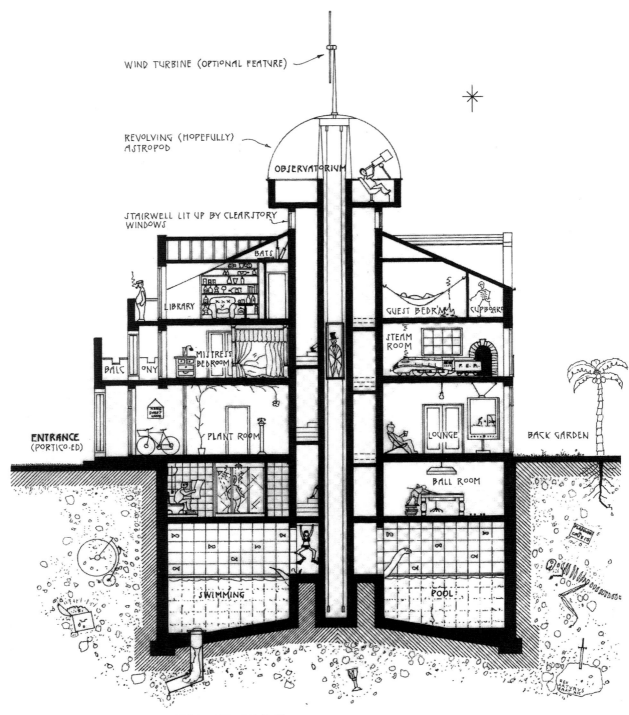

WIND TURBINE (OPTIONAL FEATURE)

REVOLVING (HOPEFULLY) ASTROPOD

OBSERVATORIUM

STAIRWELL LIT UP BY CLEARSTORY WINDOWS

BATS

LIBRARY

GUEST BEDR'M

CUPBOARD

STEAM ROOM

MISTRESS BEDROOM

BALC ONY

PLANT ROOM

LOUNGE

ENTRANCE (PORTICO-ED)

BACK GARDEN

BALL ROOM

SWIMMING

POOL

CROSS-SECTION 'E·E'
TAKEN THROUGH THE CENTRAL VERTICAL SHAFT OF THE PROPOSED ERECTION

PROPOSED: "PIG'S EAR"- NEW DWELLING REPLACING LUGG FARMHOUSE
LUGG HOLE LANE, CRAMSHAW FOLD

CREATED FOR: MR. & MRS. HORACE BELCHER

SCALE: TO BE DECIDED

DRAWING NO: 009DH-B 03

BY: DAHABLA DESIGN
C O N S U L T A N T S

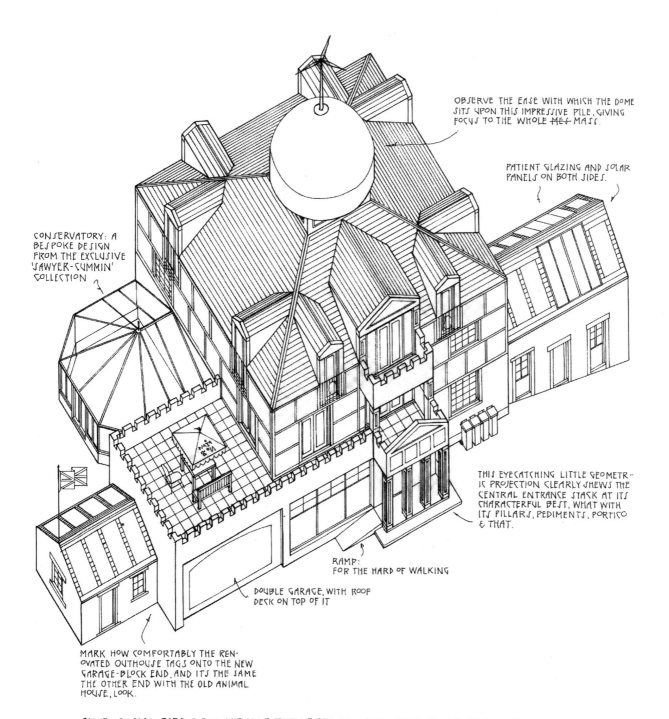

OBSERVE THE EASE WITH WHICH THE DOME SITS UPON THIS IMPRESSIVE PILE, GIVING FOCUS TO THE WHOLE ~~MET~~ MASS.

PATIENT GLAZING AND SOLAR PANELS ON BOTH SIDES.

CONSERVATORY: A BESPOKE DESIGN FROM THE EXCLUSIVE 'SAWYER-SUMMIN' COLLECTION

THIS EYECATCHING LITTLE GEOMETRIC PROJECTION CLEARLY SHEWS THE CENTRAL ENTRANCE STACK AT ITS CHARACTERFUL BEST, WHAT WITH ITS PILLARS, PEDIMENTS, PORTICO & THAT.

RAMP: FOR THE HARD OF WALKING

DOUBLE GARAGE, WITH ROOF DECK ON TOP OF IT

MARK HOW COMFORTABLY THE RENOVATED OUTHOUSE TAGS ONTO THE NEW GARAGE-BLOCK END, AND ITS THE SAME THE OTHER END WITH THE OLD ANIMAL HOUSE, LOOK.

~~AXTO~~ ~~AXOME~~ BIRDS·EYE VIEW OF "PIG'S EAR" REVEALING THE FULSOME SPLENDOUR OF IT ALL

PROPOSED:	"PIG'S EAR"- NEW DWELLING REPLACING LUGG FARMHOUSE LUGG HOLE LANE, CRAMSHAW FOLD.	**DRAWING NO:**	009DH-B 04
CREATED FOR:	MR & MRS HORACE BELCHER.	**BY:**	DAHABLA DESIGN
SCALE:	1:205·OR THEREABOUTS.		CONSULTANTS

DAHABLA DESIGN
Damien Hawkes-Blather
DipArch LRIBA

DESIGN AND ACCESS STATEMENT
PIG'S EAR, LUGG HOLE LANE, CRAMSHAW FOLD, LANC'S

1. INTRODUCTIONS
My friend Mr G Pottle, who is quite a well-known planning consultant, has asked me to prepare something called a 'Design and Access Statement' to go with the planning application he is making on behalf of his client, Mr H Belcher, and this is it.

2. DESIGN
1.3 There's not a lot to it, really. The proposed building is designed to stand as a landmark, enhancing the landscape into which it proudly and eclectically sits. Eclecticism seems to have become something of a 'persona non gratis' word among the architectural fraternity these days, which is regrettable, for one believes we should respect the styles of the past. One's scheme is thusly a medley of the new and the glories of 'yesteryear' in terms of style, balance and ingenuity and style: there's something here for everyone, surely.

1.4 The old farmhouse has to go, just look at it. But one has sought to retain and enhance two of the other ramshackle buildings on the site. The **Outhouse**, with new doors and windows to match those in the main house (q.v.), will be linked to it by a garage block, designed to resemble an animal shelter but with battlements and a big door on it. One sees this as the 'West Wing', as it were.

2.1 The 'East Wing', on the traditionally opposite side, comprises of the old **Animal House**, which at the moment has a wriggly tin roof which is neither use nor ornament. The upper floor will be lit by patient roof glazing, cleverly embracing English Hermitage's current guidance on roof windows in barn conversions. This wing successfully negotiates the change of level, keeping the building appropriately subservulent to the main house.

2.2 The Main House is artfully square in plan with its accommodation disposed of about a central staircase and lift shaft, which climb from the lower basement, to the observatorium (q.v.) which sits centrally on the roof, right at the top. The roof itself is constructed in pyramid form, with a low pitch, which prevents the building from being too overbearing in height, bulk and ugliness.

2.3 The upper part of the facades are a 'shambles', that is to say they are clad in decorative half-timbering – a conscious reference to its common usage in the construction of ~~mediaeval medaeivel~~ very old slaughterhouses, Mr Pottle's client apparently being a butcher he tells me. To give the elevation a homely, common touch of suburbinanity, reflective of quite a lot of places nearby, the panels in the half-timbered frames – like the infill between the 'Artstone' pilasters below – is in a white pebbledash render for maximum contrast and impact.

2.4 The windows proposed are of Georgian proportions and detailing to blend seemlessly with the geometry of the panelling. Frames will be of PVCu, which is just as well as they'd be a bugger to paint.

2.5 The central main entrance is a tumbling cascade of steps leading to a colonnaded portico, which in turn supports a crenellated balcony. This central edifice, with stone-type quoins mirroring those retained in the wing blocks, continues in style as it rises to break the eaves line & point playfully to the observatorium, whose pure lightness-of-being contrasts with the solidity and charm of the building upon which it appears to have settled onto. At night, a laser light display will be projected onto the dome from within, portraying the Belcher coat-of-arms. This features a wide-mouth frog squattant on gules, with bar sinister, sable and bearing the motto: 'up, down, across & polish'.

2.5 Actual accommodation is arranged on 5 main levels, with 2 levels below ground to help keep down the height of the building because it's in the green belt.

2.5 I have shown quite an expensive landscape scheme for the outside, but can we talk about that later on?

3. ACCESS
3. Access will be taken from the road.

D. H–B
x/x/mmix

The procedure by which planning applications submitted to the Grotton authorities are date-stamped, logged into the database, checked against the national and local list[2] of information required, validated, registered, acknowledged, allocated to a case officer, plotted on the GIS, consulted upon, advertised on the site, publicised, discussed internally, argued about with the applicant, re-consulted upon, completely revised following the intervention of Prince Charles, written up as a report which is then amended by the management, and occasionally lost (but not necessarily in that order) is well-known.[3]

But this is Dunromin, where process is king. Following a well-worn path, Mr Belcher's application soon took on a life of its own: the indefatigable Development ~~Control~~ Management Support Team sent letters out to around twenty-two statutory bodies (including, for reasons no one in the department could remember, the Bus Shelters Trust, the Minister for Munitions and Armaments (Wales) and the National Soap Authority) and placed a notice printed on fluorescent green paper fifteen feet up a telegraph pole adjacent to the site, explaining how local residents could have their say. Within twenty-four hours of the application being registered, full details had been uploaded to the Council's website, giving the good people of Dunromin a much-appreciated opportunity to complain about something.

The delegation arrangements in Dunromin allow the Council's planning officers to decide the vast majority of applications without any reference to the Development Management and Continuous Performance Improvement Panel – indeed, in recent years so efficient has the Authority become that in some quarters the majority of them have been determined without anyone looking at them at all.[4] This practice, while helpful in performance terms, tends to be somewhat negated by the less well-publicised fact that most applications which miss their eight or thirteen-week targets are never determined at all.

Unfortunately for Mr Belcher, his proposals were in the safest of hands: Polly Bingley may have been a slaughterer's daughter from Wagga–Wagga, but she knew a dog's breakfast when she was presented with one. It took her less than half an hour to draft a brief report for Barbara Turpentine to sign off, with a firm recommendation that planning permission be refused on policy grounds.

Gerry Pottle was nothing if not resourceful. Having a sixth sense about these things (and having also bombarded Ms Bingley with an automated e-mail, every hour on the hour, demanding to know how matters were progressing), he soon realized that things were not going according to plan. Drawing upon all his considerable experience of the *realpolitik* of the British planning system, he quickly decided that there was an urgent need to move up a gear.

The first imperative was clearly to make sure that the decision was not left in the hands of the officers. Fortunately, Cllr Catchpole, the Member for Wobberleigh West, owed him a favour, so it was a simple matter for Pottle to get him to have the application 'called in' to the Panel, on the grounds that 'I can't see what's wrong with it'. Then (demonstrating an energy, focus and attention to detail that had eluded him during his time as a public servant) Pottle set about preparing a spiral-bound, fully-encapsulated and lavishly-illustrated brochure describing in graphic terms the merits of the scheme, which he addressed personally to Mr Sheene as Head of the Service, with copies to the Ward Councillor, the local MP and (with an invitation to the opening night of the Dunromin Gilbert and Sullivan Festival) every member of the Development Management and Continuous Performance Improvement Panel. Extracts from the letter accompanying this impressive document appear overleaf:

2 In Dunromin's case, the Development Management Support Team is instructed to send back any application which is badly punctuated, puts the north point in the wrong place or fails to contain a bat survey.

3 *Source*: Local Government Ombudsman (whose unprecedented assistance in connection with the preparation of this book the authors gratefully acknowledge).

4 As we go to press, this innovative approach is being considered by the Government in relation to BAA's plans for a third runway at Heathrow Airport.

'Dear Mr Sheene,

You may remember me from the Daisy Bank Road fiasco.

My client has every desire to work constructively with the Council to secure a mutually acceptable solution to the ongoing Cramshaw Fold problem.

It would appear that your officers' reservations are based on a highly selective application of those few Local Plan policies which the Secretary of State considers there is any point in "saving" while your authority continue to make no progress on the Local Development Framework.

While I recognise that, on some interpretations, your Plan does indeed seek to discourage new housing outside existing towns and villages, such an approach must not be allowed to hinder much-needed development activity, something which is so direly needed in this great county of ours at this difficult time in our history, what with the drop in the value of the stock market and everything.

I accept that it was perfectly legitimate for your assistant to have drawn my attention to policy **ENV 8** (New Housing Outside Defined Settlements) which reads: "*New housing outside defined settlements will not be permitted*", and to the "Reasoned" Justification for the policy, which states: "*This is very important because we want to try to make sure that all new housing takes place within defined settlements, so it's obvious we have to have a policy like this one*".

My client, whose daughter happens to be a member of Friends of the Earth, fully recognises the necessity of such a policy stance, and accepts that there may well be occasions when it should be given some weight. He considers, however, that it was clearly intended to be read alongside policy **ECON 11**, which reads: "*The Council will, in appropriate circumstances, encourage proposals which support the encouragement of rural diversification (i.e. jobs)*".

In my judgment, there is every likelihood that an exclusive semi-rural location such as Cramshaw Fold would be attractive to an aromatherapist or home-based derivatives trader, precisely the circumstances envisaged by policy ECON 11. Added to which, several local lads will no doubt be employed in maintaining the shrubbery.

Given this background, I have taken steps to ensure that my client's application is determined by the elected members, and not left to the whims of temporary employees who, with the best will in the world, are unlikely adequately to appreciate its merits.

I trust your Authority will be in a position to issue the appropriate consent within a few days, since I have certain other commitments which require my presence in Thailand.'

Sheep

Mr Sheene, being a chief executive, knew little of the day-to-day artfulness of planning consultants (largely because his secretary was under strict instructions to bin anything addressed to him that appeared to have been written by one). Consequently, Mr Belcher's plans appeared on his radar only vaguely – even when letters of objection started to land on his desk from Cramshaw-cum-Wobberleigh Parish Council, the Friends of the Blether Valley and a variety of apoplectic local residents. After all, most of Dunromin's residents tended to get apoplectic for one reason or another, so he was able to take the matter in his stride.

It was not, in any event, all one-way traffic. There were strong expressions of *support* for Mr Belcher's scheme from the Grotton Federation of Small Builders (some of whose members are, in fact, quite large) and the Dunromin and District Chamber of Commerce (which Mr Sheene was shortly to address on the subject of *Financial Armageddon: How Re-Baselining can Help*: he had let slip that he was rather looking forward to hearing Bletherley Brass playing '*See the Conqu'ring Hero Come*' in his honour). Other letters suggesting that the application clearly warranted approval were from a Mrs H Belcher, Master W Belcher (4½) and a Mr Sid Pottle (whose address was given as 'c/o Her Majesty, Parkhurst, I-O-W, PO30 5AA').

This letter is typical of those sent in by the scores of objectors:

> Beau Rivage
> Bletherley Gated Community
> Blether Heights
> GR9 4BF
>
> Dear Sirs
>
> This is disgraceful. Who do these people think they are? I didn't hack my way through the Burmese jungles just so some pinko puftah of a planner can tell me what to do. This scheme does not have my vote.
>
> Yours etc.
>
> Norbert ('Nobby') Harbringer-Grudge RN OBE (Rear Admiral) (Dec'd)

A more measured response came from solicitors acting
on behalf of Mr and Mrs Figgis:

CRABBES

CRABBE & CO LLP
1 CATHEDRAL CLOSE
DUNROMIN
CHES

23 September 2009   JC / Figg / 01 / Lugghole

To whom it may concern

In the Matter of Figgis and the Bletherley Corporation

We are instructed by Mr and Mrs J Figgis, of The Manor House, Lugg Hole Lane,
Cramshaw Fold, Grotton who, being apprised of the existence of a 'planning application',
dated the 12th inst., having been duly submitted to, and acknowledged by, the Bletherley
Corporation, and who, being rate-payers of the said Corporation, do severally and jointly
OBJECT to the said application to the said Corporation (as we have said), for the reasons
which may or may not be restricted to those which are for the time being set out in the
SCHEDULE to this letter.

Yours etc

CRABBES

Schedule

that the subject application (hereinafter referred to as 'the subject application') would
result, *inter alia*, in an ineluctable diminution in the reasonable enjoyment of the
residential amenities attached to, and commensurate with, the lands and messuages
known as The Manor House, Cramshaw End, Grotton.

etc and so forth, you know the kind of thing, Miss Cribbidge

The veiled threat of unspecified legal action was, of course, the only thing that was likely to affect Mr Sheene's legendary *sang froid*, since it was a device he had himself employed to unsettle his detractors on occasions too frequent to enumerate. But Cllr Catchpole had already seen to it that the application would benefit from the careful and rational scrutiny that only the elected members would be able to provide, and so Mr Sheene's principal objective (that the blame for the decision, whatever it turned out to be, would lie where it belonged – elsewhere) was smoothly achieved. His only advice to Ms Turpentine, who had been on the point of issuing a delegated refusal, was that she produce a report which, while showing conclusively that the scheme was fully in line with the Council's planning policies, nevertheless allowed the councillors (should they prefer) ample scope to conclude that it wasn't. Or the other way round – he really didn't care.

Barbara had already concluded that Polly Bingley's assessment of the scheme was spot on. While she was disappointed to find that the County Council's Highways Development Control people had no objection (*'no surprise there, then!'* one councillor was later heard to say), she had little difficulty in agreeing with her assistant's recommendation: planning permission should be refused, for the following reason:

'The proposal conflicts with polices ENV8, GB2, ENV5, ENV6, ENV12, T2, H6 of the Dunromin Local Plan (Fifth Draft) (as proposed to be modified); policies H3, ENV1, ENV4 and T6 of the Regional Spatial Strategy for the East of England [CHECK!!]; and national policy as set out in PPS1, PPG2, PPS6, PPS7 and PPG13, in that it is a new dwelling in the open countryside outside a defined settlement, in the Green Belt and an Area of Outstanding Natural Beauty, close to an SSSSI and with a lousy access whatever the bloody engineers think. Plus the proposal would be detrimental to the visual amenities of Mr and Mrs Figgis of the Manor House, Cramshaw Fold. And it looks like a dog's breakfast' [it would appear that this reason, which is the one contained in the report to the Panel and consequently on the decision notice, was an uncorrected draft].

By the day of the Panel meeting, the number of protesters had swollen considerably (several hundred people having remembered the physical impact of Belchers' pork pies over the years). Many objectors had read *'Having Your Say'*, the Council's award-winning advice note to those planning on speaking at DMCPIP meetings. (Dunromin was initially not keen to allow public speaking, and early experiments were not entirely successful. In particular, the Council took some time to realize

that when the public are addressing the meeting, there are benefits in ensuring that they do so one at a time, rather than all at once. They also had to be persuaded by the Borough Solicitor that the spirit of the democratic process was served more effectively if people were allowed to make their contributions on planning applications *before* the Panel reached their decision, rather than immediately afterwards.)

The current protocol, the finest of its kind in the region, contains many useful tips for the potential speaker, including:

- *'it is generally best to avoid smiling'*;
- *'normally, the fact that the applicant is thought to be a Manchester United season ticket holder is not of itself a reason for opposing his application'*; and
- *'fears that mobile phone masts might cause erectile dysfunction in cats is, at best, unlikely to be accorded much weight'*.

The Friends of the Blether Valley had arrived with their faces painted bright green, singing *'We Shall Overcome'*, before establishing themselves on the front row of the public gallery, from where they proceeded to throw copies of their letter of protest (printed on gaily recycled lavatory paper) as the Panel entered the room.

After bringing the meeting up to date with the late representations, Ms Turpentine spoke briefly to explain the relevant planning policies to any members who had forgotten the relevance of such things, after which the Chairman (they don't have 'Chairs' in Dunromin), Cllr Harvey Nichols, invited members of the public to have their say.

Mrs Figgis immediately proceeded to speak for two hours and twenty minutes, quoting extensively from 'The Merchant of Venice', Barack Obama's inauguration address and the Human Rights Act (*'Having Your Say'* points out that speakers have a maximum of three minutes to make their case, so Mrs Figgis was obliged to complete her speech after the meeting had closed).

The Chair of the Parish Council urged members to reject the scheme because *'the increase in traffic on the B4878 would lead to horrendous traffic chaos on a notorious bend where a fatal accident is just waiting to happen, and will clearly bring about the complete collapse of the whole highway network, just like that dreadful IKEA the Council approved on the gasworks site, and where they still haven't done the landscaping we were promised'*.

By this time, there was little doubt that the opponents of the scheme had made a considerable impact, since several members of the Panel appeared to be in tears. Pottle clearly had to act, if his client's interests (and his fee) were to be safeguarded. He signalled his wish to speak: making the fullest use of his three minutes, he stressed the 'sustainability' of the scheme, given that the site was less than twenty minutes (albeit by car) from the nearest bus stop; he suggested that the topiary might include 'a representation of the Panel at work'; and he finished by dropping in a passing reference to Mr Belcher's fictitious war record.

The result of Pottle's intervention was a lively debate. After listening to all the arguments against the scheme and all those in favour, the Panel unanimously and emphatically *deferred* their decision for a month, pending a site visit (planning committees often do this, but generally only where it would not make it more difficult for the controlling group to come to the conclusions they had already reached in their caucus meeting beforehand).

The site visit was by all accounts a great success, despite the atrocious weather. The members had thoroughly enjoyed the way Polly Bingley had got them lost among the narrow lanes and bridle paths of the various Cramshaws; and once safely at the application site, they had continued to have fun by wandering at will over the sodden fields and watching contentedly as the Vice-Chairman (Cllr Nichols having wisely discovered he had another appointment) disappeared into an old clay pit. Some councillors were tempted to accept cups of tea (and, in at least one case, brandy) from Mr and Mrs Figgis. None was able to hear Ms Turpentine as she battled against the prevailing westerly in an attempt to yell out key points from Policy ENV8. Even the Vicar of All Souls, Cramshaw Superior turned up, albeit for the wrong case. After twenty minutes, the site visit was brought to an end, chiefly because of the growing strain on certain members' bladders.

5 It is interesting to note that the Code of Conduct gives members who feel the need to declare an interest in the outcome of an application complete freedom to choose the method of doing so which suits them best. While supporting the idea in principle, the Local Government Ombudsman has recently observed that the practice favoured by some members of winking at the Chairman just before the resolution is put, is frowned upon by leading authorities (adding that, in certain London Boroughs, it has frequently been open to misinterpretation).

Back To The Present: Decision Time

So now, the time has come for a Decision. Mr Pottle has led his client to a seat in the public gallery, just in time to see the sixteen members of the Panel file into the chamber and arrange themselves around the minimalist plywood benches, so *à la mode* in the late 1960s.

The agenda quickly reveals that Cramshaw Fold is Item 3, following consideration of an application for the change of use from a massage parlour to a Chinese takeaway in Wibberley Road, Wobberleigh, and one for the demolition of the whole of Bletherley Town Centre and its replacement with something to be sorted out later.

The Chinese takeaway is the subject of furious discussion. Members listen intently as the Council's environmental health officer tries to reassure them that, on most nights, the smells from the extraction system would be no worse than the ambient odours associated with the nearby rugby club, especially on match days. One or two of them ask the planning officer whether interpretation of Local Plan policy GEN 5, which sought to avoid the loss of valuable community facilities, could be stretched to include massage parlours; and Cllr Jim Clent is thrown out of the chamber for making a number of remarks of the type which are more generally associated with off-the-record observations of the Duke of Edinburgh. After an hour and a half, members decide to grant planning permission, subject to fifteen conditions, one of which would require the formica to be from responsibly managed sources.

The scheme for Bletherley Town Centre is approved without debate.

It is now Mr Belcher's moment. To his consternation, before the discussion starts, four members 'declare an interest' in the item and leave the chamber [this term often causes some confusion. Obviously, every councillor is sort of *interested* in the planning applications which come before the Panel, otherwise they wouldn't want to serve on it (unless of course they have been put there by their group as a punishment); and even those who might appear to be asleep during the debates are, in fact, merely thinking deeply about material planning considerations and the weight to be given to them. Having a *personal and prejudicial* interest in an item is a different kettle of fish altogether, however, especially since no one is quite sure what it means. Explaining its many ramifications is beyond the scope of this work].[5]

Cllr Mrs Blenkinsop has clearly erred on the side of caution in removing herself from the chamber on the grounds that her former milkman's mother-in-law thought she could see the application site from her bedroom window. On the other hand, Cllr Khan has undoubtedly been wise to ask the Borough Solicitor whether he had a prejudicial interest in the proposal on account of the applicant, Mr Belcher, having shoved his head down a toilet when they were at school together. (The reply he receives is *any evidence of bias would be likely to be seen by the courts as a matter of fact and degree – for example, how far down the toilet was the head pushed? Was any flushing involved?* which he interprets as the green light to stay and vote against it.) It is not clear why the other two members have left the chamber, but they appeared to be holding hands.

Barbara Turpentine introduces the item for the second time, explaining that, since the previous meeting, the Government has published a revised *Planning Policy Statement 3: Housing – What Exactly Are We Going To Do Now?* but she quickly advises the Panel that this does not affect her recommendation (while hoping that, like her, no one has read it).

It is now that Gerry Pottle plays his master stroke. He, too, has some late news:

Members, he says gravely *ought perhaps to be aware of a recent development in this case. Yesterday, my client, Mr Belcher, had an approach from an entrepreneur who wishes to establish an organic pig farm on his land. This would involve the rebuilding of the existing structures and their change of use to the storage of rotten turnips; and the erection of another building up to 465 sq m in floor area for the housing of extremely organic pig slurry. The 5000 or so pigs would, of course, be free to roam at will through the surrounding countryside.*

I have informed my client that the proposals appear to be "permitted development" under the appropriate regulations. I have further advised him that adding an associated methane-fuelled power plant and an eco-visitor centre would be clearly supported by a number of policies in the Regional Spatial Strategy and the Tokyo Accords. I am also dealing with a number of enquiries for a wind farm, a Retreat for members of parliament and several mobile phone masts.

Members may conclude that such developments would be unlikely to be received with unqualified approbation by many of their constituents – that, of course, is not a matter upon which it would be proper for me to comment. I am, however, instructed to say that, were the Panel to grant permission for the modest residential development the subject of the present application, my client would be willing to enter into an agreement under S106 of the Act which would ensure that an appropriate accommodation could be arrived at …

Upon hearing this, Mrs Figgis falls into a dead faint (Pottle makes a mental note that, were he to get his planning permission, he would be in a perfect position to advise her about challenging the decision in the courts). Several councillors are heard to say that they haven't a clue what Pottle has been talking about, but most seem to have a rough idea – and the reference to methane has clearly put the wind up a number of them.

The time is now 12.55. Cllr Nichols, wondering why on earth he ever agreed to be the Chairman of the Panel, senses the nervousness of some of his colleagues. More importantly, he wants his lunch. But he seems to know something that no one else does … From the top pocket of his waistcoat he draws out a folded piece of paper – a handwritten note given to him by Barbara at the Chairman's briefing. *Members,* he says *I have here a piece of paper, a note prepared for me by Ms Turpentine …* and before Barbara can stop him, he proceeds to read it to the meeting:

It's quite possible that Pottle will try the smelly organic piggery threat again (you'll remember Daisy Bank Road, I think). By my reckoning, he's used this on at least five different sites in the last twelve months. Every time he's been bluffing. The bloke's an idiot. Take no notice.

Right … he booms, waking up the young reporter from the *Grotton Advertiser*, *… you've all read the report* [guffaws from the public gallery] [and from some of the officers] *and you've been out on a nice trip in the bus. I am sure little purpose would be served by any further debate. All those in favour of the planning officer's recommendation that permission be refused, please show.*

*Most Planning Inspectors still find the Decide-o-Matic Mark III
quite a useful tool*

At this point, Cllr Bunting (who, it later transpires, owns a similar ruin to Cramshaw Fold in the adjacent field) wakes up, or nearly so. Cllr Bunting is something of a fixture in Dunromin's corridors of power: he was first elected to the old Bletherley Rural District Council in 1951, but appears not yet to have mastered any of the procedural niceties of debate. His great strength is that this has never bothered him. He therefore starts out on a lengthy exposition of the desperate need for tasteful new housing of the type now being proposed and why he can see nothing wrong with Mr Belcher's scheme, Mr Belcher being a long-standing supporter of the local bowls club.

Before Cllr Bunting can get properly into his stride, however, the Chairman gently explains that the motion has been put, and that the debate is over. Again, he bellows: 'All those in favour of accepting the planning officer's recommendation please show'. Members of the Panel are seen glancing furtively at each other, before first one, then two hands are raised. 'All those against?' Again, two hands go up! (there is also a distinct 'guilty as charged' from Cllr Bunting). 'Are there any abstentions?' Somewhat sheepishly, all the remaining nine councillors, raise their hands (although it is possible one just wants to leave the room). What now?

Cllr Nichols is a seasoned campaigner. He has not got where he is today by taking any unnecessary risks with his political capital – which is why he has always made it a rule never to commit himself unless he has to. Now that he is faced with the casting vote in this perilous situation, he is determined not to make it count. The concept of 'the precautionary principle' has always appealed, and that is what leads him, 'with some reservations', to opt in favour of accepting the officer's recommendation.[6]

The blood has drained from Mr Belcher's face. He asks his consultant what all this means. 'Not to put too fine a point on it, old chap' says Pottle, 'we're stuffed'.

****

Post-scriptum: at the time of going to press, Gerry Pottle has persuaded his client to lodge an appeal to the Secretary of State. His grounds of appeal, to which he states he will add when he has read the Council's response, are 'It's always worth a shot'. He has asked for a public inquiry.

6 The fact that the application site lay within the highly marginal Cramshaw St Peters ward which he had the honour of representing was, as he later confirmed on Radio Chirpy, neither here nor there.

A quiet corner of Grimethwaite

chapter five
Regeneration in Crisis

General Overview

Back at the time of the previous Planning in Crisis Conference in 1979, regeneration in Greater Grotton was just getting into its stride. Up to that point, it had largely been a question of knocking things down and starting again, but more sophistication had developed. Houses were being rehabilitated, and people were even being consulted about how (as the jargon has it) to shape their own places.

At that time, Grotton County Council could raise vast resources simply by putting a penny on the 'Rates', and nobody could stop them. To improve the lot of their citizens, they were doing things like reclaiming slag heaps, trying to attract jobs, and subsidising minority interests such as opera and bus travel. This intolerable situation was, of course, terminated by the Government in the 1980s; their concern that Councils might raise money and spend it on things people needed has been well documented.

For a time, Councils were told by Ministers that they did not have any role at all in economic development. Today of course it has become a priority, with all kinds of encouragement and exhortation, hoops and hurdles provided by a benevolent Government as a substitute for actual cash. Long-standing Grotton councillors, now being instructed to do something which, not so long ago they were instructed not to do, and not so long before that did of their own accord, fully accept that whatever they do next is likely to be the opposite of what the Government of the day think they should be doing, which itself will be the opposite of what the Government used to think they ought to have done ages ago (but now should have stopped doing).

During the 1980s, regeneration in the County was patchy, despite the initial success of the Grotton Garden Festival (visitors to the city can still see the remains of the Japanese pavilion, somewhat overwhelmed by the lush remnants of their innovative Knotweed display). Efforts to attract a Toyota factory to Golden Delicious foundered in the face of competition from elsewhere, and the inability of Ministers to locate the District – which, as usual, was not returning phone calls and had not yet got round to ignoring e-mails. An Enterprise Zone was created in Muckthorpe, to which reference is made later, and a proposal to create an early Urban Development Corporation got as far as a statement from the then Mr Heseltine that 'the UDC in Grimethwaite has been an outstanding success', put out shortly before the idea was abandoned.

Even Cloggley, generally thought to have weathered the industrial shake-out better than most, had had its problems. The main source of employment in the town had long been a warehouse from which Cadogan and Grosvenor's world-famous organic rejuvenating body balm was distributed around the globe. Available in handy 10 ml sachets, these proved impossible to open in modern showers, especially if you had false teeth, and this had begun to affect sales badly. The company folded completely when the product's Chinese manufacturers (neither Cadogan nor Grosvenor having been directly involved nor, indeed, having actually existed) were shown to have used as active ingredients not buttercups and wild sorrel, as they had claimed, but linseed oil and dilute sulphuric acid.

Dunromin, of course had no need of any regeneration initiatives.

Throughout most of this period, where regeneration projects were carried out, they were considered to be a simple matter of breathing new life into clapped out land and buildings and providing new Job Centres; whereas today it is much more about things like tackling obesity, and saving the world, although not necessarily in that order. Just in time for the 2010 Conference, therefore, regeneration has 'grown up'. The main indicator of this is its incomprehensibility. The immense complexity of the modern industry, which defeats even its most devoted adherents, and certainly those engaged in the planning of Grotton, is a challenge to everyone involved.

The Government has done its best to keep the country at the cutting edge of best practice in this important field, primarily by ensuring that the many rules, guidelines and targets with which Councils have to comply – together with the names of the initiatives themselves and the 'delivery vehicles' required to, er, deliver them – are regularly swept away. Several of the organisations which are important in regeneration will have been abolished, amalgamated, re-titled or rebooted between the authors' index fingers hitting these keys and the words appearing on their screens, though in due course most of them will be re-invented with different titles.

It is for this reason that key current programmes such as 'Towards Prosperous Communities' and 'Excellent Places, Exceptional People' are soon to disappear (if the White Paper 'Tip-top Towns, Spiffing Suburbs' is to be believed). So experienced have Grotton's planners become in keeping abreast of the welter of initiatives with relentlessly optimistic names launched by Government (sometimes on a monthly basis) that the ~~Polytechnic~~ University (pending) have recently doubled the size of their School of Theoretical Administration – an example of successful regeneration in itself.

In Chapter 1 Professor Sulkie drew attention to T Break's personal mastery of this newly emerging discipline, through the creative use of his Scrabble expertise. Grotton was indeed fortunate in having Break at the helm during that critical period. Such talent is difficult to replicate. This is especially the case in Grimethwaite, where the problems of regeneration are so stark and so pressing. Wayne Blunt (whose proclivities are of a less cerebral kind) has at times had to struggle to prevent his blighted Borough from descending even further down Lonely Planet's list of the Hundred Worst Places in the World. The battle to rescue Muckthorpe Bottoms makes for a sobering case study …

Muckthorpe Bottoms

To say that Muckthorpe Bottoms is in need of regeneration is like saying the sea's wet, or that Jeremy Clarkson needs a lethal injection. There are, amongst other ghastly things, a former gas works, a bombed-out bone-crushing plant, and several million tonnes of indeterminate material, thoughtfully distributed over a wide area by local builders as a way of reducing the need for landfill. The canal houses a unique ecosystem dominated by supermarket trolleys and old bikes; and, symbol of Grimethwaite's fall from grace, the ornate Italianate tower of the former Parnassus Mill, topped now by a substantial mobile phone mast, presides over the area, rather as the single lingering rotten tooth of a dying tramp might crumble in his decaying gums and barren, rancid mouth.

There is some sign of life: deep in the gloomy recesses of the semi-derelict buildings and railway arches, Grimethwaite's more adventurous residents can find cheap lino and frangible furniture, body building clubs, and 'photographic studios'. Out along the B5098 sits the main, indeed the only, achievement of the Enterprise Zone: six grey sheds, grouped randomly within a sea of tarmac, punctuated occasionally by a dead shrub. Built originally for 'non-food retail warehousing purposes', they now moulder away, damp ridden and decaying, surrounded by the north's most varied assortment of broken glass, colourful condoms, and a selection of unusual weeds.

A more recent arrival is Radio Chirpy, Grimethwaite's local station, which occupies the sixth floor of another old mill. '198LW CHEEKY CHIRPY'S CHEERY CHAT', is the legend on the chimney, though the missing 'C' in 'chat' is a source of grim local humour. DJ Dave has become something of a folk hero since he aligned himself with the campaign to preserve the best of the area's heritage; his souped-up canary yellow Golf can usually be seen happily blocking the entrance to the mill yard, a symbol of defiant entrepreneurship in an otherwise desolate and largely abandoned industrial wasteland.

On the edge of the area, two small communities stagger along. A group of Victorian houses in the Southern Bottoms, centred around Sebastopol Street ('Little Crimea'), somehow survived the slum clearance programme of the 1960s, and one of Messrs Bettabuild's first speculative developments around Windermere View ('The Lakelands') now provides students of building surveying from the ~~Polytechnic~~ University (pending) with classic case studies of rising damp, dry rot and rodent infestation, to say nothing of periodic inundations from the adjacent River Grime (which are generally held to improve the appearance of the area).

Things could not go on like this. Over many years the Council had sought with little success to bring succour to the Bottoms; but things were getting worse and now Wayne needed to act.

The Big Push

In 2005, Alexander Quibble from the Government Office arranged a tour of the area in the company of Tristram Hampton, from the Regional Development Agency. Hampton, 29, smooth as silk, his manner urbane, his voice loud, his confidence abundant, his hair coiffed, his teeth gleaming, his shoes burnished, his salary high, was reluctant to venture too far into the Bottoms for fear of chemical damage to his Ozwald Boateng suit, so they drove around the edge of the area in one of the RDA's several 4x4s, and surveyed the scene of desolation through binoculars from the top of the Co-op. Then they repaired to the Municipal Offices for a discussion. The minutes of the meeting make interesting reading:

Grimethwaite circa 1840

Minutes of meeting held on 1 November 2005
Committee Room 3, Municipal Offices, Grimethwaite

Present
Alexander Quibble *Regional Director, GO*
Tristram Hampton *Associate Director Business Transformational Benchmarking, RDA*
Wayne Blunt *Borough Planning Officer, Grimethwaite Borough Council*
Courtney Blunt *Grimethwaite BC (minutes)*

Meeting commenced 2.30
Mr Hampton said that in his view Muckthorpe Bottoms was in a bit of a mess, and suggested that the Council should consider some kind of regeneration programme.

Mr Blunt said that this had occurred to the Council already; in fact it was the reason why he had asked for the meeting. He had noticed on his frequent visits to the photographic studio that the area was a bit run down, even by Grimethwaite standards.

Mr Hampton said that he thought it would be necessary to produce a plan for the future of the area. Mr Blunt produced a series of such plans, going back to 1975, but Mr Hampton instinctively felt that these were of little value, saying that he personally knew a particularly suitable firm of architects in Oldham who could turn their hands to planning and would do a good job.

After a short pause to fiddle with his Blackberry, Mr Hampton said there would also be a need to consult the people who live in the area. Dad offered to put him in touch with Mrs Paradigm, who ran the local residents' group, but Mr Hampton felt that the use of a particularly suitable firm of Public Relations Consultants which he personally knew in Stockport would be the best route to follow.

Mr Blunt assured the meeting that the Council stood ready to do whatever was necessary to ensure the success of the project. Mr Quibble and Mr Hampton both indicated that the Council would have only a limited role. The seriousness of the situation now demanded that an Urban Development Corporation should be formed, but the Council would be allowed to nominate a member to attend Board meetings. An officer in the Development Control Division would need to give permission for whatever the Corporation wanted to do. Mr Hampton made it clear that as it was the RDA, and not Grimethwaite, who had access to 'shedloads of wonga', it would be best if they went along with it.

The meeting ended at 2.40

Quibble advised Council Leader Sid Spriggs to take this as a compliment; UDCs, or at least the cash they brought with them, were much sought after. Most people had to settle for an 'Urban Regeneration Company' which, as he understood it, was similar but without the 'wonga'. A Board was formed, comprising mainly local agents and developers. Unfortunately most of them left when they heard a talk from the Audit Commission on 'conflicts of interest'. This had never been a problem before in the Grotton area – indeed it had been the foundation of the local economy – but 'better safe than sorry' seemed a wise motto in the circumstances.

It was quickly determined that the UDC would be formally established by 1 January 2006. Immediate benefits were realised when a welter of jobs was created, including a project manager, a hands-on programme director, a contract negotiation and client-side intercommunication supervisor, a spreadsheet preparation executive, a floor target monitoring administration officer, a milestone identification manager, a creative business partnership and stakeholder liaison director, a risk assessment and attenuation planning officer, a head of exit strategy preparation, and a clerk. Targets were set, including the erection by 3 February of 200 colourful banners displaying the UDC's motto 'Bottoms Up!'.

So far, so simple. But Wayne had once read a copy of 'Regeneration and Renewal' (a journal for the more ambitious sort of planner) and knew there were other ways to bring more money to the Borough. As a result a 'Pathfinder' was set up to knock down the Southern Bottoms, and a 'New Deal for Communities' initiative was established for the Lakelands Estate. Wayne was also trying to get to grips with Business Improvement Districts (BIDs), Local Housing Companies (LHCs), New Growth Points (NGPs), and any other initiatives he might have missed while his back was turned. Such was his zeal for bringing useless chunks of the alphabet to the Borough that he even toyed with the idea of declaring a Simplified Planning Zone (SPZ). This was a measure of the desperation attaching to the area, but even in the extreme case of Muckthorpe Bottoms it was impossible to see how such a move could be of the slightest benefit. However a European office was opened in Brussels and Mlle Amélie Coquette was appointed as Grimethwaite Plenipotentiary.

In addition, Wayne was encouraged by Quibble to open discussions with Grotton City Council about the possible formation of a Multi-Area Agreement (MAA), or possibly an Economic Prosperity Board (EPB). He was slightly in awe of Nicola Tilbrook, but nonetheless approached her in a spirit of co-operation. Negotiations proceeded slowly, but there was agreement in principle that both Authorities wanted to make things better rather than worse, and this provided the basis for further discussion.

A bigger problem was emerging for Wayne however. The necessity to attend meetings of the UDC, the Pathfinder Board, the New Deal for Communities Board, the negotiations about the MAA, BID, SPZ and EPB, and various Euro-meetings, together with the need to talk to the Homes and Communities Agency, the Commission for Architecture and the Built Environment, the Environment Agency, Natural England (re the orchids), and many more left him little or no time for running Grimethwaite.

Nevertheless, he was able to make a particularly positive and dynamic contribution to a meeting of the Local Strategic Partnership. His detailed proposals regarding the role of the Grotton and Cloggley Constabulary in tackling breaches of the advertising regulations were well received. It was only later that he realised he had been at a meeting of the UDC Board where the debate was supposed to be about a transparently futile plan for a new tram system. Since everybody else was similarly confused about which meeting they were at, his error remained undetected.

The Local Strategic Partnership

The Government has not, for a couple of decades, issued any advice or guidance which has failed to mention partnership. This is something it widely advocates though, for itself, it prefers a more unmediated approach. Grimethwaite's LSP is responsible for producing the Sustainable Communities Strategy (SCS), which emerges perfectly formed by a process of osmosis, and for implementing the Local Area Agreement (LAA), which is an agreement to do what the Government says.

It had taken Grimethwaite some time to come to terms with this new style of operation, and indeed the LSP was still feeling its way. Obesity, health and terrorism were not matters the old development plan had tackled directly, but in these new days of 'spatial planning' it was clearly important that it should.

The LSP set about its core business of setting, agreeing, and monitoring targets and indicators, including:

- *Average girth of teenagers*
- *Mugging rate*
- *Increase in teenage pregnancy rate (negative increase preferred)*
- *Attendance at over 65s belly dancing classes*
- *Acts of Terrorism per 1000 population*
- *Average temperature increase at Grotton Airport*
- *Number of homes lacking en suite facilities*
- *Graffiti – percent improvement in grammar and spelling*
- *Faith communities: persons remaining awake during Bishop's sermon*
- *Drugs: propensity to snort (excluding Council members)*
- *Something about jobs*

Though most of these targets have so far not been met, the separate objective to produce not less than 2500 pages of impenetrable monitoring material per annum has been exceeded by a substantial margin.

The Work of the UDC

Meanwhile the Board of the UDC was going about its principal business of organising meetings. Led by little Hampton, who transferred from the RDA, it engaged a fleet of consultants from outside Grimethwaite. Naturally they determined to prepare a master plan which, by definition, contained the following standard requirements:

- *the Spine Road*
- *the Iconic Structure*
- *the Opportunist Initiative*
- *the Unwanted Apartments*
- *the Gay Scene*
- *Training and Skills*
- *The 24-hour City*
- *Creative Industries and*
- *Gentrification*

Looking at each of these in turn:

The Spine Road

Obviously there has to be a Spine Road, and this one can be seen clearly from the Co-op roof, bisecting the Bottoms from north to south – a masterpiece of the road builder's art which can be appreciated all the more as a result of the complete lack of development along its length. The line of elegant trees, the perfect pavements, the nugatory pedestrian crossings, the profligate street lighting and the cycle path which ends in the canal – all these are an impressive sight. At intervals precise junctions are provided, promising easy access to who knows what, who knows when, who knows why?

The Iconic Structure

At the very first meeting of the Board it was decided that there must be an iconic structure. It was explained that this was a *sine qua non*, which Wayne thought was a movie which nobody watched, but in fact was described in all the regeneration textbooks as an essential ingredient. It was to be one of the seven wonders of the modern world; it was to put Muckthorpe on the map, to bring hope and opportunity. The spin-offs, said the consultants, would be too time consuming to calculate, but would probably involve the creative industries in some way.

A competition was held, attracting entries from some of the world's greatest artists and designers. The Board quickly dismissed the idea of a bloody great model of a white horse – someone else has fallen for that since – and also the proposal for a pile of scrap metal from Frank Gehry. An idea to recreate the idea of the Hanging Baskets of Babylon was more attractive, especially since there had been no entries in the 'Grimethwaite in Bloom' Competition since its inception in 1958, so the UDC might immediately win an award, which would be good for morale.

But the eventual winner was the Colossus of Muckthorpe, designed by Audrey Grumpie, from the Faculty of Certifiable Arts, Crafts and Zoology at the ~~Polytechnic~~ University (pending). This giant piece, more than 500 feet high and standing astride the B5098, would not only be beautiful but practical. The observation decks in its nipples would give views of the whole of Greater Muckthorpe, weather permitting (meteorologists predicted that clouds would cover the upper parts of the sculpture, which would have its own microclimate, on about 100 days a year). The bungee jump from its outstretched index finger would be a major attraction (and the children's alternative located at the tip of its slightly aroused penis was a master stroke). The Royal Navel Museum would complement these attractions, while the nostrils would operate as a waterfall and could also be used by caving enthusiasts. Energy to power the internal Maglev system, which whisked visitors to the merchandising opportunity in the Adams Apple, was to be supplied from the World of Waste.

This has not yet happened.

The Opportunist Initiative

Grotton Academicals, the football team of choice for all local supporters, had come a long way from their days in the old Hanseatic League Division 2, and now played in the Barings Bank 4th Division. They aimed to emulate the big boys of regional football like Hyde Rangers and Atletico Dukinfield and were keen to attract new investment and relocate from Cowpat Park, their old ground near the centre of the City of Grotton. There was obviously a unique atmosphere at the Cowpat, though the Environmental Health Department were able to trace that and serve the appropriate notice. The ground failed to meet FA standards for the Barings League, the two jumpers being placed at either end ten minutes before kick off being seen as somewhat outdated in the modern high speed world of ~~ruthless commercial money dominated exploitation of innocent fans~~ football.

A fresh start was clearly needed, but the proposal to relocate the stadium to the Bottoms was opposed by Grotton City Council. The emotional attachment to the stadium was intense; fans especially recalled the twinkling feet of 1950s star winger Wee Jimmy Jinkie as he dashed up the wing, before being deposited in the River Bogg by opposing centre halves hewn from the local gritstone. The Council also wanted to retain the economic benefits of match day, when pie sales quintupled. Its opposition was inhibited, however, by the fact that all the Councillors were season ticket holders, and therefore couldn't vote on the issue, even though nearly all the tickets were fully paid for.

The UDC sought to take advantage of the situation by pretending they had thought of it first, and putting together a funding package, including the proceeds from the development of the old ground (if the City Council would accept an alternative use, such as a bike shed). The Academicals, sponsored by Help the Aged, aimed to 'take the club to the next level' (understood to mean upwards rather than downwards though this is far from clear) and were hoping for big things from their advert in the *Grotton Advertiser*:

Club Chairman Bert Stott MP (who, fortuitously, is also a member of the UDC Board) said: 'We don't think it's totally unrealistic to see ourselves as becoming the Middlesbrough of the south west Pennines – though without the sea of course, and without their obvious advantage in terms of heritage and cultural history. We can dream.'

The scheme under consideration by the UDC contains, it will be no surprise to learn, a small stadium (500 capacity), to be shared with the local Rugby League Club, and a 50,000 sq metre superstore. In view of the objections from the City Council a Public Inquiry is anticipated.

This has not yet happened.

The Unwanted Apartments

Before the credit crunch, Messrs Bettabuild provided a small block of flats with tiny rooms and 'breathtaking views of the historic River Grime' (as they put it, even though the Grime was in a culvert at that point). Aimed at the Muckthorpe buy-to-let market, which proved to be non-existent, the flats are empty. This puts Grimethwaite in the regeneration mainstream.

Further blocks are proposed, but this has not yet happened.

The Gay Scene

It is received wisdom that there is a direct correlation between regeneration and homosexuality. Unclear as they were about the mechanics of this juxtaposition (and reluctant to delve any deeper), the Board nevertheless decided that a lively gay scene would bring benefits to the Bottoms, via 'the Pink Pound'. Bert Stott felt that the damp climate was unsuitable, but nonetheless a grant was agreed for the establishment of an appropriate club by the canal and no further questions were asked.

This has not yet happened.

Training and Skills

The UDC was soon made aware of certain gaps in the local skills base. Reading and writing spring to mind. The production of a series of leaflets aimed at local people (How to Produce a CV, Interview Techniques, How to Make an Omelette, Polo for Beginners) failed to engage hard-to-reach sections of the community, though the advice to businesses (How to Get a Grant for Something, How to Lay People off) was more successful. Currently the UDC is seeking to persuade the ~~Polytechnic~~ University (pending) to relocate some of its courses to Muckthorpe, including the renowned School of Bouncing Studies,[1] whose graduates will be invaluable if the 24-hour city ever materialises.

This has not yet happened.

The 24-hour City

Acutely aware of Grotton's success in this regard, the UDC determined that Grimethwaite needed to be a 24-hour city. This ambition, which meant an addition of approximately twenty-two hours to the previous daily span of activity, seemed to involve people sitting out on the pavement in the winter under huge patio heaters wearing very little, drinking lager cooled to near freezing to disguise the complete lack of flavour, and throwing up outside nightclubs much later than had previously been possible.

But this has not yet happened.

1 Bouncers have been one of Greater Grotton's few
  areas of employment growth in recent years.

The UDC's vision for the future of Muckthorpe Bottoms

Creative Industries

The existence of Radio Chirpy and the 'photographic studio' seemed to the UDC to provide a possible focal point for the development of creative industries. It would be impossible for the UDC to hold its head high at any regeneration gathering unless it could demonstrate success in this field, and there were boundless celebrations when a web designer set up business in a disused substation, applying the latest cyberspace techniques to prototypical network applications (i.e. working in porn). Of course the Colossus will also attract a wider cross-section of artists and designers from all over the world, subject to it being built.

This has not yet happened.

Gentrification

The improvement in the Southern Bottoms is seen by the UDC as a success story. The Area Gentrification Programme has begun to attract movers and shakers such as the Academicals' star player, the Croatian Dragan Prosaič, and a man who works in fashion. DJ Dave, from the Chirpy Breakfast Show, has also shown his faith in the area's future: he lives on the corner of Sebastopol Street, next to where the local shop (now a wine bar) used to be.

All this has enabled the UDC to tick several boxes on its spreadsheet (one of its targets was to attract at least one Waitrose van a week to the Bottoms and this has now been achieved). It has however come as a disappointment to those responsible for the Pathfinder programme, who'd been looking forward to knocking the whole area down and starting again.

For the UDC all this is a mixed blessing. The rising value of the quaint two-up, two-down and two-bits-shortly-to-be-built-on-what-used-to-be-the-backyard properties has put them beyond the reach of local families. Even worse, the incomers have formed a residents' group dedicated to keeping the industrial heritage of Muckthorpe unchanged. 'Save the Bottoms', as demonstrated later, has already become a thorn in the side of the UDC.

Funding the Colossus

As everyone involved in regeneration knows, there's capital money and there's revenue money. Unfortunately for the Colossus project, up to now it has neither.

Naturally the UDC had been relying heavily on dubious S106 agreements to pay for the scheme, but due to the collapse of the local property market this now appears to be a lost cause. Grimethwaite and the Community Infrastructure Levy go together like a horse and ski jump. The regeneration model based on private sector investment is, thought Tristram, broken and since he had known no other model in his short life he was bereft of ideas. Tesco had promised to pay for the buttocks, but beyond that the prospects were poor.

The Government said it had no resources either, and was running out of ways of re-presenting old money to make it look as though it was new. The lottery was being used for the Olympics, but Europe had often been a source of cash for lost causes and the UDC began to investigate, despite the Euro scepticism of Bert Stott, who muttered something about fish and bent bananas, or maybe bananas and bent fish. Mlle Coquette was pressed into service.

The relevant programme proved to be the Programme for Integrated Landbased Enhancement Solutions (PILES), or its successor PILES PLUS. It was, it seemed, necessary for Muckthorpe to form an association with like-minded communities in other member states, and though the Board would have preferred somewhere warmer, the officers eventually settled for more kindred sites amongst the east German lignite mines, somewhere in Lithuania, and a nuclear waste store in Poland. This Association of Rather Mediocre Places in Trouble (ARMPIT) submitted a joint bid for funding, based on allegedly complementary projects of widely varying character.

Tristram rapidly got to work on laying the ground for a bid. He confidently predicted its overwhelming success, and ultimately his own progression to higher things. He advised the Board that six accountants would be needed to put the bid together, but that the cost of this could be 'capitalised'.[2] To gain the Council's support, he said that the same helpful device could be used to provide in-kind contributions to the salaries of the Chief Executive and two secretaries, plus office costs, a car and a chauffeur, half the cost of running the Planning Department, rent for the use of the Town Hall, and a daily crate of Perrier water. Unfortunately however there was to be only one project officer to develop and implement the scheme.

Of course targets for the sites were developed, as required. EU officials spotted that the annual number of visitors predicted for the Colossus (300,000) was probably an overestimate by a factor of at least 100; however Tristram argued that if you included drivers viewing the Colossus from the M62 (from which it could be seen with the aid of simple binoculars) the number of visitors would be well into the millions.

The amount of land to be reclaimed was surprisingly small, comprising only the feet, entry booth, bungee jump landing area, and ambulance station. But a substantial number of jobs would be created. Naturally there was to be a full complement of staff exchanges and seminars to swap experience with other Colossuses, and disseminate the results of the developments.

As far as the future running costs were concerned, Tristram was equally confident that the scheme would 'wash its face'. The exit strategy involved leaving behind a fully functional Colossus, self-financing through parking charges and the sale of teas and recycled Structure Plans. It would be free to enter the site (though there would be a hefty charge to leave), and in a joint venture with the nearby World of Waste, leachate from the site would be recycled to make a nourishing French Onion soup.

2 Another word for 'fudged'.

Other ARMPIT partners had parallel, though different, targets. But a hiccup afflicted the exit strategy for the Polish nuclear waste store, as the 10,000-year half-life of much of the material sat uneasily with the EU's rule that grants should extend no more than five years ahead.

The views of Grimethwaite's Planning Committee were mixed. Wayne managed to convince them of the value of the Colossus itself quite easily. However the essential large sign with the EU logo and extensive text in twenty-five different languages, thanking the Convergence and Regional Competitiveness and Employment Objectives Funds for their generosity, proved a problem in planning terms (though the fact that it would hide most of the Bottoms from Muckthorpe Town Centre was clearly an advantage). There were health and safety issues as well, with fears that in a strong wind it could take off and provide a serious threat to Huddersfield.

EU dignitaries paid a site visit, and the locals steeled themselves for the inevitable succession of interminable speeches. There was a shortage of Michelin-starred restaurants in Grimethwaite, and indeed in the County as a whole. Even in Dunromin, there was only one chef who had ever appeared on television, and that was on Crimewatch. However, an on-site picnic involving Lancashire hotpot eaten out of a selection of European newspapers proved a huge success.

The bid has not as yet been successful. Nonetheless the UDC has commenced the construction of the Colossus, and at the time of writing has got as far as the left knee. Several problems have emerged. The only textbook on Colossuses, Pliny the Elder's description of the specimen at Rhodes, though full of romance, lacks detail when it comes to engineering and construction. Muckthorpe finds itself at the cutting edge where, as ever, all estimates of cost are hopelessly inadequate. The responsible Minister, whose reputation is at stake, has set a target of reaching the groin by the next election and has indicated that she will 'look again at sources of funding' (which, in English, means switching cash from other worthy schemes) if that is achieved.

Stakeholder Involvement

It is an essential feature of regeneration, and indeed of planning as a whole, that local people are consulted on what is proposed, ideally before it has been agreed. The Bottoms was no exception.

The problem for Mrs Paradigm, of 17, Windermere View, who was Secretary of the Muckthorpe Federation of Residents' Groups, was the sheer scale of consultation. During a typical week she would receive bundles of documents from the Council, the UDC, the Pathfinder Initiative, the New Deal for Communities, the Environment Agency, Messrs Bettabuild, and various double glazing companies. She had given up her job at the toy shop, had her letter box widened, built an extension to house the paperwork, and divorced her unfortunate husband.

Her routine never varied. The mammoth postal delivery would arrive at Windermere View (or the Primary Distributor, as she now knew it was officially called) at the crack of lunchtime. She would open the packages and expertly scan the latest consultants' reports or revised master plan. Unimpressed by flashy drawings, she would home in on flaws in the household formation calculations, and could even manage a wry smile at the assumed turnover/floor-space ratios. But she never lost sight of her key objectives: no matter how many times she was asked whether she favoured a high, medium or low-growth strategy, or what she thought of the methodology of the environmental appraisal, she always replied that the bus service was poor and that there was nothing for young people to do.

Most days, she would attend the LSP, or the Partnership Board, or the UDC's Consultation Forum (at which Tristram would patronise the locals at length over a plate of fish and chips), or some other meeting. There were also exhibitions to attend, meetings with European visitors (she had been offered and accepted an unpaid job with the UDC as 'Token Local' for these purposes), letters to write to the *Advertiser*, and the shopping to be done. Usually there were evening meetings with one or other of the regeneration agencies covering the Bottoms.

Mrs Paradigm's vision was not shared by 'Save the Bottoms', who were a different kettle of ointment. After surviving the Pathfinder's demolition ambitions, the group managed to persuade the Council to declare a conservation area covering all the streets around Balaclava Terrace and Sebastopol Street. Values in 'Little Crimea' went through the roof, and a lecturer from the ~~Polytechnic~~ University (pending) moved in.

But, having shown their faith in regeneration, residents began to get nervous. They opposed the construction of the Colossus; the notion of charabanc-loads of people from Barnsley looking into their front windows through the telescope in the left nipple was disturbing. They feared the noise from the 24-hour city, if it ever transpired; they worried in case the football hooligan moved to the area; and they were nervous about the creative industries (which might attract advertising executives, thus lowering the tone even further).

So they began to oppose planning applications for any activity which might affect their way of life, which apart from the odd Albert Roux franchise and a nice country park, was most things. Though the UDC was able to deal with this in the normal way (by ignoring it), STB were a thorn in their side without which they could well have done.

The Bottoms Today

The Bottoms today very much resemble the Bottoms yesterday, and the Bottoms the day before. The UDC has not matched the achievements of some of its sister organizations elsewhere, despite the best efforts of Tristram Hampton, the support of Mrs Paradigm, and the encouragement of the Council. There have been several reasons for this. The demise of Messrs Bettabuild and the rest of the private sector was always going to be a problem. The opposition of the Environment Agency, who saw a river and envisaged a flood, has been a difficulty. 'Save the Bottoms' continue to be an effective group. But, most of all, Muckthorpe Bottoms had fallen so far, sunk so deep, that traditional solutions involving thrusting young things with hair gel and a lot of flats were just not going to be enough.

Dragan Prosaič limbering up at the Academicals training ground

Rural Cloggley: the never-changing pastoral scene

chapter six
The Countryside in Crisis

Crammed as they are in metropolitan Grotton, many of the County's residents may not use their countryside very often but they feel better knowing it's there and hope it will always look as it did 200 years ago – like Hovis, or Bobby Charlton. Indigenous countryfolk may have special needs, unhelpfully pressing for the preservation of basic rural services like post offices and EU grants; meanwhile those who made their fortunes elsewhere before finding their rural idyll devote their time to old country traditions like blocking footpaths, setting fire to ramblers and objecting to planning applications. Given this potentially explosive mix, the future of Grotton's countryside is uncertain – and is yet another challenge facing the county's planners …

Grotton's Rural Areas:
A Theoretical Analysis

'Like all great conurbations, the County of Grotton is a complex amalgam of town, country and lots of in-between bits that academics down the ages have enjoyed giving a complicated name to.' The famous geographer-planner, Sir Peter Hall, did not include this observation in his seminal handout '100 Random Facts you need to Commit to Memory if you want to pass Geography O-Level', but he might well have done.

Surely Johann Heinrich von Thünen got it right when he jumped out of the bath one evening in 1849 exclaiming: '𝕸𝖊𝖎𝖓 𝕲𝖔𝖙𝖙, 𝕯𝖗𝖊𝖎 𝕽𝖎𝖓𝖌𝖊𝖓!!' (neatly eclipsing his compatriot Wagner, who could only manage ein). Von Thünen's flexible tool, thus revealed, has proved invaluable in understanding the three broad types of countryside in the county.

First encountered, as one leaves the bustling city, is the notorious *urban fringe*. In Grotton, the County Council is desperate to convince local residents that this uninspiring landscape, of boarding kennels, electricity pylons, unauthorised tips, decrepit Shetland ponies, algae-filled ponds and schoolchildren studying the habits of hedge-dwelling mattresses and the distribution of supermarket trolleys, contains all they need for a jolly interesting and sustainable day out. However, the Council's perpetually under-resourced Countryside Management Service, with its assortment of volunteer students, young offenders and pensioners whose wives don't want them under their feet, generally struggles to persuade visitors that pond digging in the local sewage works is more rewarding than getting in the car and taking the dog for a bit of sheep worrying in the National Park.

Blether Valley Country Park is seeing the benefit of recent investment

Beyond the urban fringe, and forming the next of Von Thünen's concentric rings, comes the *nice countryside* within reasonable commuting distance of the city centre and increasingly sought after by the urban stressed who can just about survive the rural tranquillity, provided they are furnished with a decent dual carriageway to get them back to the office or the theatre in twenty-five minutes flat. An uneasy relationship with the agricultural community is often in evidence – the incomers' default position is that the countryside is best seen, not heard. Or smelled.

Heinrich's third ring is represented in the county by the *outermost hilly regions* of rough grazing, peat bog and characterful wind farms to the north and east of Cloggley. Some of this is now in the new National Park and some is not. It takes a skilful planner to tell the difference.[1]

National Planning Policy for the Countryside

The Government's approach to development within the rural areas of the kingdom is not always expressed as clearly as it might be; it is therefore hardly surprising that it is being interpreted in a number of different ways on the ground – often, in Grotton's case, on the same bit of ground and all at the same time. This has led to some confusion locally, as this parliamentary exchange illustrates:

MEMBER FOR CLOGGLEY: Does the Minister have plans to visit Cloggley in the near future, or at least when the floods have abated, because if he does, he will appreciate that my constituents benefit enormously from the Government's current rural planning policy as a model of wisdom and clarity? And could he remind me what it is?

MINISTER: I am delighted to assure my Honourable Friend, the Member for Clopley, that the aspirations and concerns of his constituents are never far from the Government's thoughts. They will be reassured to know that I shall shortly be issuing a new interpretation of the relevant Planning Policy Statement (PPS), whichever it is now.

The first and most important objective must of course be the promotion of a vibrant rural economy based firmly on a robust agricultural sector, not forgetting the need to afford equal priority to the conservation and enhancement of the countryside, where the vigorous promotion of public access for recreation remains key to dealing with obesity and stuff – subject to an assurance to farmers and landowners that they can maximise their productivity without interference. It is also crucial to the future of the nation that our rural areas play the fullest part in helping us to meet the challenging targets for the provision of renewable energy, though this should not of course be at the expense of the landscape, especially in areas such as the Honourable Member's constituency of Coddley, where I have recently learned I have one of my second homes.

Above all, it remains crucial to the Government's vision for the countryside that new housing be made available of the right type, in the right place, at the right time and in the right place, without there being any discernible impact on overstretched local services, the landscape or people's feelings. Moreover, the Government is committed to as much of this housing being affordable to local people as is consistent with its other policies, or most of them, but not so much as to distort the operation of the market, or limit the freedom for people to live where they wish, except where there are other people who, for whatever reason, don't want them to.

Given the Government's long-held view that decisions affecting the lives of local residents should always be taken locally, it is for the local authorities to set out the steps they intend to take if these goals are to be achieved. I am satisfied that, given the initiative that I have announced today, and our continuing willingness to urge councils such as Clogton to do better, all these objectives can be met without the slightest difficulty.

I also take this opportunity to announce a forthcoming review of our countryside agencies with a view to establishing whether there is a need for yet another helpful body with no funds.

Sorry, I should have mentioned minerals somewhere.

(Sits. Cries of bravo, yer, yer, etc.)

MEMBER FOR CLOGGLEY: Er, so, will you be visiting Cloggley?

1 Given the tendency to locate the less desirable activities just outside the park boundary, this may change with time.

English Heritage has put Cloggley's ancient Moot Hall on the Buildings at Risk register

Cloggley's Approach to Rural Planning

It will be seen therefore that the Government's confidence that all things are possible in the best of all possible worlds relies heavily on the actions of local councils. Nowhere is this more true (or less interesting) than in Cloggley, where Peter Rabbit struggles amiably to satisfy the conflicting needs of all of the Borough's diverse 'stakeholders'.

Rabbit knows that *landscape assessment* lies at the heart of planning in the countryside and involves different firms of landscape architects (or different landscape architects from the same firm) disagreeing about what can or can't be seen from particular viewpoints, and what difference it would make if you could. If the landscape character assessment of the area is 'integrated', that's much nicer and carries more weight. (Weight in this context refers not to the size of the individual landscape specialist but to the number and volume of appendices he has felt it necessary to produce at the public inquiry.)

Armed with the fruits of this *assessment*, Cloggley's planning policies have long sought to offer sustenance to the dwindling band of farmers who cling to the Borough's rural tracts like water to a duck's back. Not everyone agrees that the policies have worked in the way intended. In particular, Rabbit accepts that the Council has generally been too easy-going in assessing applications for *agricultural workers' dwellings* in the open countryside.

Some of the arguments used by applicants to justify new houses, and accepted by his team in the past, are now widely seen as errors of judgement (even where they have included such cutting-edge green technologies as rain-powered barbecues and tidal jacuzzis) – for example, the Council has now admitted that it regrets having allowed a number of on-site dwellings because of the alleged need to bring the more sensitive crops indoors each night during the coldest weather. A more rigorous approach to this controversial area of policy is likely in the future.

Farming is not yet dead in Cloggley – the area has more silos than the Civil Service – but few believe that it will survive in its present form more than a few more years. That is why attention is turning increasingly to something called *rural diversification* as a way of avoiding dealing with the issue, with the area's potential for tourism high on the agenda.

Perhaps the most *célèbre* of several recent *causes* in the Borough is American Krunchy Kreme magnate Ronald Crump's scheme for the creation of an eight-hole pitch and putt links course, with associated 750-bed hotel and conference centre and 500 holiday villas, on the area's famous shifting spoil heaps. Though located on the Ayrshire coast in the 1950s, these now lie some 200 miles to the south in Cloggley.

Opinions continue to be divided on the merits of this controversial proposal. There was vigorous opposition to the scheme based on the unique geological qualities of the Site of Special Scientific Interest and the seasonal presence of a bearded tit, but the promise of highly regarded jobs in the ball finding and hotel bed turndown sectors was sufficient to win the necessary majority in the Planning Committee. The first hole has been dug but, owing to economic downturn, work on the site has now ceased.

An agricultural worker's dwelling in Cloggley

Rural Regeneration: The Cloggley Way

In addition to its statutory planning role, the Borough Council has taken a lead in promoting rural regeneration. It can't, of course, do this on its own and, with the County Council, defra, GO North West and local business organisations, has launched the 'CLOGGLEY SECOND' rural development partnership (unfortunately the name 'CLOGGLEY FIRST' was already in use by a local dry-cleaning firm).

CLOGGLEY SECOND has begun to implement an ambitious programme of capacity-building, co-operative marketing initiatives and IT support (Spittle now boasts what is believed to be Britain's only milking shed based internet café: Daisy the Cow's Facebook home page had over 900 hits last year). So successful has this programme been that every second farm now offers a traditional Cloggley afternoon tea with choice of Earl Grey or mild, a genuine heritage experience helping to muck out the llamas and a fascinating maze created from abandoned tractor tyres. An EU funded programme, 'AGAs for AGA', has stimulated the local woodland sector by installing wood-burning ovens in schools throughout the County. This has brought a whole new meaning to the term 'match funding'.

CLOGGLEY SECOND has also promoted the establishment of farmers' markets across the county. Unfortunately there were soon more markets than farmers, and everyone who wanted a scented candle or organic shampoo already had one. Indeed, the trade in candles from unsustainably managed sources has become something of a local scandal: in the lawless Pennine foothills of Cloggley the trade is now dominated by cartels and the local edition of the *Advertiser* has featured a number of articles on jojoba running and ylang ylang rustling. Nonetheless, the three new jobs created in the candle sector have gone some way towards mitigating the past thirty-five years of decline in the land-based economy as a whole.

And the County Council?

The County Council itself has continued to adopt a high profile in support of the rural community across the county. While it has admittedly been obliged to close most of the rural schools and withdraw all subsidy for rural bus services, on the positive side it has been able to deploy a two-man team to clean road signs every four years in each parish.

Its annual Rural Enterprise Award was won this year by farmer Maris Piper, who explained her success:

> 'We've put 10 acres into Entry-Level Stewardship, we're laying about thirty acres down for paintballing and another thirty for quad biking, and we're planning to put down a nice Center Parcs over on Ragwort Common. The judges particularly liked our Travel Plan, with the opportunity that the new bike rack provided for our Walter to cycle to work from Dewsbury.'

The County Council has also taken direct action by giving preference to locally sourced foodstuffs in local schools and the County Hall canteen – though doubt has been expressed about whether this really was intended to cover the whole range of crisps from the supermarket in the High Street. 'The brie in the cheese and onion is definitely local – it just isn't local to here', as it was explained to the Council's Scrutiny Committee.

Somewhat fitfully, the County Council convenes and services a countywide Rural Stakeholders' Forum comprising the great and the good – and a few who aren't so special, to be honest. During closures of the rights of way network due to crises like foot and mouth, bird flu and the locally virulent alpaca minge, the County Council, recognising its ongoing responsibilities for footpaths and nettles and seeing the severe impact of the closures on the rural economy, made full use of this Forum for the purpose of securing rural votes. While the response of the agricultural community has been a little disappointing, farmers do at least tend to send more interesting Apologies to the meeting, usually involving being stuck in large machinery or ruminants.

The Pipers' award-winning farm now recycles its hot pig slurry in a highly successful beauty treatment business. It is vital that the unguent is kept at 65°F – the temperature it comes out of the pig

The National Park

The evocatively named *South West Pennines National Park* was designated in 1982, and confirmed in 2008 following a comparatively brief public inquiry. (The Inspector's recommendation was touch and go until, in line with Natural England's designation criteria, she recalled a *'markedly superior recreational experience'*[2] with a fireman in the hills above Spittle whilst on her undergraduate planning course.) The discovery that the new organisation would in fact be a brand new planning authority taking over some of his 'patch' rather caught Peter Rabbit unawares but, on reflection, he thought that might on balance be no bad thing as he wasn't getting any younger and, well, if someone else wanted to have a crack …

The new National Park Authority has recently finished recruiting, and the thirty-one staff of its Barn Conversion Division are already hard at work. While perceived by supporters of the National Park as a cure for all known ills, and a few unknown ones as well, the Authority is not proving universally popular, especially with anyone keen to improve the signal to their mobile phone, put a roof on their property or paint the front door. The Authority's standard condition on all planning permissions for satellite dishes, for example – that they be faced in natural gritstone – has divided the local community, as has its requirement that all staff should be locally sourced, sustainably managed and zero carbon.

In regular correspondence with the Park Authority has been the paramilitary wing of the *Keep the National Park National* group which is pressing for the repatriation of all invasive species including Himalayan balsam, the sycamore and chicken tikka masala.

We'd better say something about minerals.

In the distant past, a number of minerals were worked in the upland areas beyond Spittle, probably by Cistercian monks, and generally without the benefit of planning permission. Today, the only significant mineral extraction in these areas takes the form of quarrying for high quality building stone, for which there is a continuing demand, on account of the large holes which they tend to produce, into which all sorts of interesting material can later be tipped. The County Council's responsibilities for minerals planning have now passed to the Park Authority, whose recent efforts have focused on attempts to negotiate the termination of some 300-year-old permissions which, because of the rather lax control regimes prevalent in those days, could over a period of years result in the removal of the entire Pennine chain and its redistribution around the M25. The Authority's emerging core strategy seems certain to come out against this.

2 Go to www.planning-inspectorate.gov.uk/southdowns/
   documents/SouthDownsRe-openedProof.pdf
   et many *al.*

Cloggley is very serious about sustainable transport

chapter seven
Transport in Crisis

Historical Perspective

There is plenty of evidence to suggest that the Romans, with their usual astuteness, ensured that they could get out of Grotton as quickly as possible by building roads in all directions.

An illustration taken from the Technical Appendix to the first Legionary Transport Plan (LTP) indicates the likely position of the main routes in the vicinity at about AD 68. Some scholars are hopeful of discovering a further route to Bath, but others believe that, while plans were undoubtedly drawn up and Side Road Orders drafted, the efforts of a veritable *Forum* of local amenity groups, combined with the discovery of a Maximus Crested Newt on the line of a proposed slip road, were sufficient to derail the project (though for understandable reasons this was not the expression used at the time).

And that, in effect, was more or less it until the great days of turnpike building also passed the area by. Not one carriageway realignment or build-out was constructed between the end of the Roman occupation and the halcyon days of road scheme postponements in the 1960s.

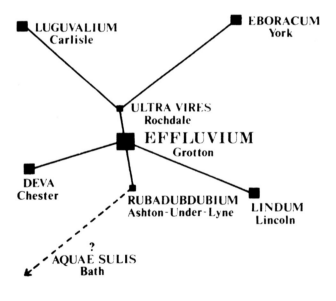

Roman roads around Grotton, c. AD 68

Current Government Policy

There is no clearer explanation of the Government's current transport policies than that set out in a recent answer to a Parliamentary question. Grimethwaite MP Bert Stott had emerged from the Members' bar, as he was required to do on a regular basis, to simulate concern about the lack of investment in transport in his constituency. The Minister involved[1] answered as follows:

First I would like to remind the Member for Grimethwaite of the Government's transport strategy, which is of course based on affording the highest priority to addressing the current problems relating to the global environment which, I am the first to accept, are an inconvenience for my Department. For centuries it has concentrated its efforts on trying to get people quickly from one place to another in their motor cars. This has proved a popular course of action and I am reluctant to diverge too far from it merely because of what we hope are temporary climatic problems. We must continue to support the British economy, which is largely dependent on huge trucks traversing our motorways at high speed.

It is true that more recently we have been urged to build high speed railway lines. This of course would be of little benefit to the Member's constituents, who one imagines could rarely afford to travel on them, or indeed on any of the current trains, if any remain operative in his constituency. The funding system for trains not only reduces the amount the taxpayer provides, but also increases the profits available to the entirely excellent railway companies. Unfortunately there is always a loser in these otherwise splendid arrangements, and in this case it is of course the passenger; but this only increases the need to concentrate on road building.

Unfortunately, with available transport funding needing to be constructively re-optimised, it has been suggested quite mendaciously in some quarters that the creation of more and more labyrinthine processes to be negotiated by highway authorities to secure funding is a mere device to divert attention away from the fact that almost nothing is actually being built. In many Councils of course this would in any event occur; the introduction of senior staff with management qualifications rather than professional expertise – while it has helped in ensuring statistical returns are expeditiously manipulated – means the actual building of things assumes a lower priority.

Nonetheless, we have set out to simplify the process by which transport funding allocations are made.

As set out in the Local Transport Act 2008, all highway authorities now have to produce a new Local Transport Plan by the end of March 2011, except where they don't. In areas with Integrated Transport Authorities, which for the avoidance of doubt are metropolitan areas and other areas (not metropolitan areas) which wish to form themselves into Integrated Authorities, the responsibility to produce a Local Transport Plan rests with the Integrated Authority, and the constituent authorities (unitary or metropolitan district, and any authorities in other areas where an Integrated Authority is formed) do not have to produce one, because there'll already be one. Elsewhere, for clarification, they do.

The improvements outlined here will complement the parallel and highly successful rationalisation recently undertaken of governance at regional level, bringing together the strategies and bodies responsible for planning, transport and economic development under one organisation solely interested in economic development.

Authorities will still be expected to produce an annual progress report on delivery, which Government Offices always enjoy reading.

Councils should continue to demonstrate their strategy for delivering the provisions of the Road Traffic Reduction Act – unless they find it inconvenient or are getting stick from local business or motoring organisations.

'Whatever happened to Accessibility?' I hear you ask. I can hardly re-emphasise frequently enough that this remains an important plank in our policy armoury. So much so that I can announce today that I have set up a working party to examine the issues relating to this vitally important topic, and have instructed it to proceed with all speed and report on its suggested draft terms of reference by the end of next year, or thereabouts. I will naturally keep the House informed of progress, if any.

1 Whoever he or she was: as with most such Ministers, only weeks passed before his or her demise and the mists of obscurity, already thick, turned into a dense and impenetrable fog of inconsequentiality.

It was no surprise that the Minister failed to answer the question about lack of actual investment in Mr Stott's constituency. However, exciting first steps have been taken to deal with some of these problems. There was dancing in the streets in October 2009, when the Government announced that funding for Phase 4 of the Grimethwaite sub-Regional Inter-Modal Minimum-Cost Transportation Infrastructure Package Longitudinal Feasibility Study (known affectionately by the planners involved as GRIMMCTIPLFS4) would be placed in Priority Band 2 (and not 3, as the Council had feared) in the Department for Transport's next spending review. Progress, indeed.

There has also been rejoicing at Grotton's Ryan Giggs International Airport. It seems that the way is now clear for approving the extension of the runway by thirty-five metres into the Green Belt even though the plans have yet to be drawn up. This is because the scheme will now be considered by the IPC. Quite why the publishers of *Woman's Weekly* and *Amateur Gardening* should be the appropriate body to decide these important matters is unclear, but City Councillors who see the airport as crucial to Grotton's international competitiveness are convinced that the windsock is now pointing in the right direction.

Alexander Quibble, at a recent meeting, denied that the IPC was a mere rubber stamp. They would of course be able to approve the development, but not until a National Policy Statement supporting it had been prepared and this may take some time. As he put it:

> 'Any NPS has to go through various hoops and hurdles which have been erected, no doubt assiduously, by my Civil Service colleagues in the public interest, before Parliament – in its infinite wisdom – considers the matter. Others of my colleagues in a sister Department, who will have to negotiate the hoops and hurdles thus so carefully erected, may have cause to regret that assiduousness, though, de profundis, any ensuing delay in the preparation of the policy can only be for the public good.'

It is of course true that not everyone welcomes the anticipated fast track approach of the IPC. The legal community for example are concerned that it is proposed to operate without the manifold benefits of their particular contribution to the development of public policy. As Charles Silke QC opined:

> 'What, may one enquire, might be the purpose of having highly-trained, hugely intelligent and generally handsome lawyers if they are not permitted to perform the function for which they alone are uniquely qualified? It is beyond peradventure that ruthless, elegant and, where appropriate, interminable cross-examination is central to our long-established principles of fair play, public scrutiny and exorbitant fees. It has worked perfectly well for centuries and I submit that no credible evidence has been adduced which could reasonably be said to support a conclusion to the effect that it might fail to perform a concomitantly necessary function well into the future. That will be 250 guineas.'

The Local Dimension

Meanwhile, the wind of change has been blowing through County Hall, and not only because of the shortcomings of its original concrete and asbestos construction. Despite the sophisticated traffic modelling of the Roman era (the abacus is still to be seen in the Cloggley Museum), Grotton in the 1970s was struggling to cope with the latest techniques. The Department of the Environment's insistence on modelling the effects of the Ipswich–Worksop–Clitheroe motorway on traffic flows in the eastern part of the County, proved tricky. Especially as they claimed they didn't intend to build it. And even if they did it wouldn't affect Grotton.

Real progress was only made with the arrival on the scene of Donald MacDonald. MacDonald, now the County's Director of Transport and Environment, cut his design teeth in the late 1970s on a scheme to solve the problems of traffic congestion in Slattocks, protect and enhance the special qualities of its Conservation Area, and at the same time slash thirty-five seconds off the driving time between Oldham and Ashton under Lyne. Though Donald regrets that the completed bypass has yet to be connected to any other part of the road network, his faith in its ultimate value is undiminished. See pages 98 to 100.

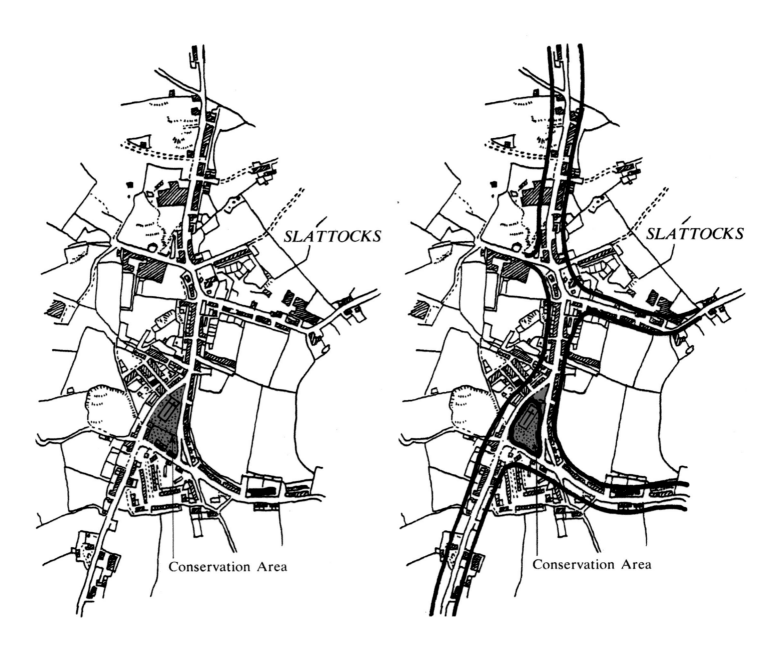

1. *The design problem: the character of Slattocks and its historic conservation area is threatened by heavy traffic on the B6041*

2. *Original proposal by the former Slattocks UDC (abandoned 1975)*

SLATTOCKS

SLATTOCKS

Conservation Area

Conservation Area

3. Scheme advocated by County Planning Department and therefore rejected by the County Engineer

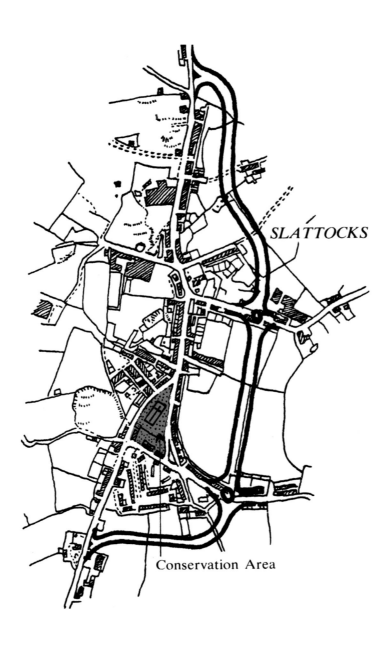

SLATTOCKS

Conservation Area

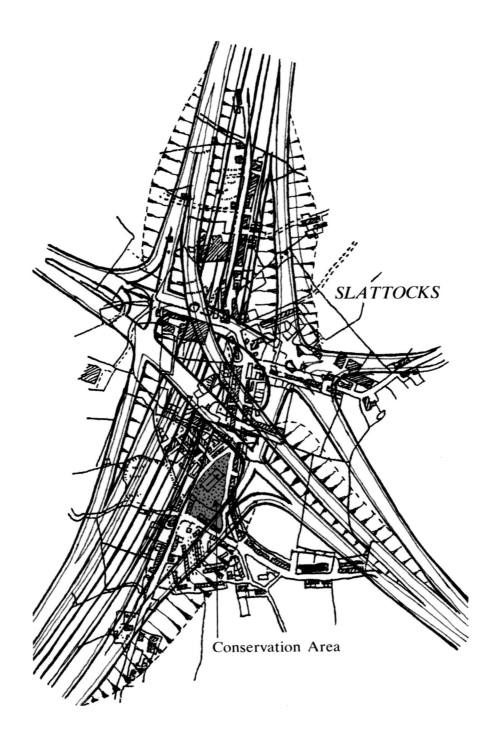

SLATTOCKS

Conservation Area

More recently, Nicola Tilbrook has had a number of tense conversations with Donald about the possibility of setting up an 'Integrated Transport Authority' for their combined area, hoping for support in the City's ambitions for major investment in transport infrastructure to facilitate its plans for regeneration. Her aim is to see investment in the next two years on a series of bus lanes, park and ride schemes, and a ludicrously expensive light rapid transit network. At their last meeting, and to Nicola's surprise, Donald fully supported this approach – subject to the substitution of four-lane dual carriageways for bus lanes, and grade-separated junctions for the rapid transit.

Consultation by the transport planning authorities during the development, implementation and monitoring of the LTP has become ever more sophisticated. With the emphasis now very much on 'engagement with local delivery partners', through the 'Local Strategic Partnership',[2] there is now no need to meet with the actual public in draughty village halls and be shouted at. This is just another example of the County's streamlined commitment to community empowerment: when rural bus services are cut, for example, local people are empowered to fend for themselves.

A recent extensive consultation undertaken jointly by the County, City and Districts on the possible introduction of charging for on-street parking in the city centre produced a resounding 'no' vote which will mean going back to what used to be called the drawing board: transport planners at the City and County attribute this to the failure to agree a consistent form of wording in the consultation. The leaflet authorised by a majority vote of AGA bore the words:

> *'Bearing in mind the frightening implications of climate change for future generations and the horrendous prospect of unlimited all-day traffic chaos, would you be prepared to pay a token amount for on-street parking, or would you insist on pursuing a selfish and highly unsustainable lifestyle?'*

Dunromin, however, circulated its own version reading:

> *'Would you prefer to be able to continue to drive into the city centre and park just where you want for as long as you want for free, or pay through the nose for it?'*

Transport Planning in Action: A case study – the Sustainable Ring Road

Thanks to the Freedom of Information Act two notes of a meeting held to discuss one of the 'missing links' in the Grotton Outer Ring Road, or Sustainable Link, as it is now labelled, have been released. These help to demonstrate how the Grotton authorities co-operate on delivering the transport infrastructure to support today's complex economic, environmental and social agendas.

The first of these had been produced by MacDonald, in his office in County Hall, with its collection of Top Gear DVDs and model racing cars.

Note of meeting 21 March 2010

Purpose of meeting: to persuade City to support 'Missing Link' at Regional Partnership Board

Present: Nicola Tilbrook *City*
Tom Culvert *City Engineer's*
Self
Koffi Break

NT outlined City initial 'position': priority is park and ride site just across boundary in Sheene's territory, with bus and bike lanes along radial into city centre, plus traffic calming, real time bus inf, etc, etc!! All v well meaning of course. Impressive intellect but doesn't grasp essentials.

KB predictably flaky on this but explained need to demonstrate to Govt Office that we're making links between econ perf and good t'sport (i.e. road!) links. Can only achieve Air Qual aims by building Missing Link, free-flow traffic, etc.

Culvert clearly on-side and is working on NT – think we're getting there.

Explained that current scheme has trees, porous surface, etc, and offered to add 'sustainable' to scheme title. Some haggling. Promised dual carriageway badger underpasses plus innovative network of o'head wires for dormice disguised as power lines to blend with l'scape.

Next steps: dig out orig version and work up for submission. Brief Lead Member on need to say nice (not too pos!) things at AGA re City's t'sport ideas.

Resolved – Top priority – Link Road – we can both support at AGA and Regional Board

Donald MacDonald takes no chances with highway safety

The second meeting note had been written by Tilbrook in her Town Hall office, distinguished by its range of UNICEF posters and her battered bicycle.

Meeting note 21 March 2010: To discuss priority schemes for submission to Regional Partnership Board

Present: Donald Mac and K Break
Self and T Culvert

D Mac outlined County position. Amiable enough. Enormous feet! But still pursuing old Ring Road scheme! Peddling the old 'build our way out of congestion' line. Bit more 'green' window dressing than last time – but same old same old.

I explained (again!) our emphasis on sustainability, public transport, equalities, DDA, etc, etc; need to align with clear govt priority on climate change. No chance of supporting major h'way construction. Culvert not all that supportive – must speak. D still committed to building something before he retires – pref connected to the network this time!!

Resolved: top priority is combined package of sust transport measures which we can both support at AGA and Regional Board

Transport Planning in Action: The Soft Alternative

While major highway construction is something of a rarity these days, despite the unshakeable enthusiasm of Donald MacDonald, there has been an increasing emphasis on measures aimed at forcing, or conning, people out of their cars.

An example is the first phase of the Real Time Bus Information system, which has been put in place in case any money is found later to help run some buses.

A trawl of items on the City's Planning and Transport Committee agendas for 2009 reveals reports from Nicola Tilbrook on the following: Workplace Travel Plans, School Travel Plans, Personalised Travel Plans, Toolkits, Car-Sharing, Parking Charges, Demand Management, Road User Charging, Congestion Charges, Quality Bus Partnerships, Real Time Information, 'Community and Voluntary Transport', Rail Development Strategies, Humps, Bumps, Build-outs, Public Realm, Bike Priority Measures, Safer Routes to School, 20 mph Zones, Air Quality Management Areas, Walking Strategies, Car Free Day, Bike2Work, Modal Shift, Travelwise, TravelChoice, Smart Measures, 'Quality of Life', Equality Impact Assessments, Transport Innovation Fund, and Obesity.

Sadly, it appears that the Do-Nothing option is the optimum fit with current budget estimates.

Conclusion

So what is there to learn from Grotton's experience? On the surface all is sweetness. But underneath, the age old struggle between the unreconstructed hard men of the County and the Department for Transport, with their giant diggers and token trees, and the gentle pragmatism of the environmentalists, with their pedestrianisation and Peruvian knitwear, is being resolved in the usual way. As we go to press the City Council is considering funding a guerrilla group established to hurl insults at 4x4 drivers outside schools; while the County is considering adding a couple more lanes to the inner relief road. *Plus*, as they say, *ça change*.

chapter eight

The Environment in Crisis
or What's Posterity Ever Done for Me?

At the time of Grotton's last great Planning in Crisis Conference in 1979, the Environment hadn't been invented: delegates simply had to make do with Geography.

The idea that members of Grotton's Development Control Committee had to take account of the destruction of the polar ice caps or the realignment of the gulfstream would have seemed faintly risible.

But now it is clear, as night (for the time being anyway) follows day, as the rising flood waters of fate meet the hurricane-damaged electricity cables of destiny and the consequent explosion sets fire to Birmingham, it will play some part in our lives, like it or not. The weather – or climate, as we must learn to call it – is changing. Admittedly the tourism department thinks vineyards in Dunromin and year-round topless sunbathing in the Spittle sand workings might attract visitors to Grotton (for the first time); and the longer term prospect, brought about by rising sea levels, of Grotton resuming the coastal location it last enjoyed before the Ice Age would be of some benefit to the struggling local shipbuilding industry (as outlined in Chapter 1). However, for reasons way too complex to explain here,[1] climate change is thought to carry with it a number of potential problems, including the end of the world.

Responses to climate change are essentially twofold and everyone must play his or her part. Local initiatives are key: advice from the *Grotton Advertiser*'s Weddings, Wine and Environment correspondent, Anthony G Fyson, for example, reads as follows:

*You should **adapt** by:*
- *Getting your trip to the Maldives in before they drown*
- *Swapping your thermal vest with someone who hasn't been listening, for a thong, unless the gulfstream stops, in which case you will need a parka*

*And, like Sting, you should **mitigate** climate change by:*
- *Ticking the carbon offsetting box on every third flight*
- *Remembering not to put those used yogurt pots in with the ordinary plastic for recycling*

It is the local authorities who bear the greatest responsibility for ensuring that future generations will inherit a sustainable, liveable or, at least, extant Greater Grotton. Their responses to this crucial question have varied, of course, but as always there are valuable lessons to be learnt.

Dunromin

The Royal Borough of Dunromin sees itself as a front-runner in this field. Utter commitment to the cause of fighting climate change has been the watchword of the administration for several years now.

The driving force behind this is the Leader of Dunromin Council, Sir Hartley Hartley-Wintergrene, 72. Sir Hartley, who was knighted in 1987 for his services to tweed, is a retired estate agent, with all the social standing and intellectual kudos which that status implies within the Conservative Party. Normally Jeremy Sheene spends much of his valuable time stopping

---

1 See *The Cub's Guide to How to Earn your 'Save the Planet' Proficiency Badge*.

the Leader from saying anything too embarrassing, but his writ does not run to the political arena. We reproduce here a speech which Sir Hartley delivered at a fringe meeting at his Party Conference in 2009 which eloquently summarises his approach to environmental policy.

'I am grateful for the opportunity to address this great conference on the subject of environmental issues. Dunromin has an environment and we are very keen to keep it just the way it is. As a Council, we are determined to be as successful as the party is nationally in explaining how we will deal with such looming crises as global warming. The difference between us and the other parties is that we intend to do this without in any way inconveniencing the indigenous people of the Royal Borough who have voted for me at every election since 1978 and, colleagues may wish to note, have made my seat the safest in the north west.

We can truly claim that environmental issues lie at the very heart of our corporate processes in the Authority. We base all our policy making on the well-known three-legged stool – the environment, the economy, and whatever the other one is. We see no reason why the economy and environment shouldn't go hand in hand, like gin and tonic, or polo and pretty gals!! You know, sustainability isn't just about pointless self-sacrifice, wearing hair shirts and making empty gestures, although all these have a part to play. It's about choice and win–win situations, and using the right words to make it look as though we're doing something.

We carried out an extensive survey of public attitudes to environmental issues and lifestyles across the Borough. Almost everyone who responded said they were in favour of improving the quality of life, the only exception being the Chamber of Commerce. Dunromin residents, apparently, are not in favour of having a lot of new houses built in the Borough because well, there just isn't the water, and it would lead to pressure on things called aquifers and more hosepipe bans, which nobody wants.

It is the Authority's belief that the greatest contribution the Borough can make to dealing with the big issues of the day is to remain the most attractive of places to live and work so that others might have something to aspire to. The extremely high car ownership and usage have helped avoid the need for highly polluting buses. The removal of height barriers at all household waste sites has enabled access for the larger SUVs, thus trebling the rate of garden waste recycling. We also do our bit by measuring how much paper and energy gets used in the Town Hall – though I'm afraid I can't remember why. And we do have a dual-fuel car in our vehicle fleet – I understand it works almost as well as any other car. Delegates will have noticed the arrangements I made to be seen looking approvingly at it outside the Conference venue.

We can only hope that Johnny Foreigner is doing as much! My fact-finding trip to the Arctic proved it's still jolly cold up there, which I'm told is only as it should be.

We have been criticised in some quarters for objecting to the park and ride site proposed within our boundaries. It needs to be understood that this would be entirely for the benefit of people for whom we are not responsible. I can hardly imagine any of our people making use of it! I do not see how it helps if we try to stop Dunromin residents from driving to their private parking places in the centre of Grotton. Do they want the place to be regenerated or not? Why, oh why, is it always the poor motorist who gets it in the neck?

Ah, I see I've a note here to mention something called "carbon trading", and that it's a jolly good idea. Well, if those chaps and chapesses over in Grimethwaite need any for their barbecues, I'm sure we are more than happy to sell them some. Win–win again!

Well, anyway, we must be doing something right. I can tell you that the weather in Cramshaw Superior has hardly changed over the past ten years.

Does anyone have any questions?'

Dunromin's demonstrable commitment to green principles has been rewarded by a rapid increase in the number of applications and enquiries for renewable energy schemes, and particularly for wind turbines, singly and in clusters. Somewhat alarmed at the thought of the likely response from Dunromin residents, the Council rapidly included an appropriate policy in the emerging core strategy:

> **Policy ENV44:** *There will be a presumption **against all proposals** for the generation of energy from non-fossil fuels of a scale in excess of 5 kw, other than where the environmental benefits, including generation of energy to be derived from the proposal, clearly outweigh all the many environmental disbenefits including, but not restricted to, national, regional or local issues of landscape, visual impact, fauna and flora, recreation, heritage, culture, noise, air quality, flood risk, coastal defence and householder amenity.*

Jeremy Sheene spotted that this wording could, if taken the wrong way, appear a trifle negative in the current climate. He instructed the planners to come up with a new policy which left no room for doubt as to the Authority's green credentials. After considerable drafting and redrafting, the following has now become the new policy:

> **Policy ENV44:** *There will be a presumption **in favour of all proposals** for the generation of energy from non-fossil fuels of a scale less than 5 kw, other than where the environmental benefits, including generation of energy to be derived from the proposal, are clearly outweighed by the many environmental disbenefits including, but not restricted to, national, regional and local issues of landscape, visual impact, fauna and flora, recreation, heritage, culture, noise, air quality, flood risk, coastal defence and householder amenity, or may have the potential for being a disbenefit, or are located, or may be perceived to be located, within 10 km of any watercourse, or that might on a good day be visible from any classified or unclassified road or dwelling, other than a travellers' site – and certainly not if it's anything at all nuclear.*

Clearly a major step towards sustainability and this approach now runs like a very runny thing throughout the Council's plan making.

Dunromin requires its residents to sort their weekly recycling by grape type

Grotton City

Nicola Tilbrook's brisk vegetarianism, her immaculate allotment, and her solar powered exercise bike are signs of both her enthusiasm for, and her Authority's commitment to, the green agenda. Environmental considerations inform each and every aspect of its work. Every house is zero-rated, every drop of rainwater is to be used to flush the loo or directed to a Sustainable Drainage System (SUDS), every roof is to be green and the Authority has installed solar panels on all Council buildings (unless permanently in the dark, like the Human Resources section).

Nicola has been obliged to acquire a basic understanding of at least one new eco-friendly technique a week for saving energy, or generating energy, or managing waste, all guaranteed to be the next big thing – in order to be able to advise the Council and keep its planning policies up to date. She has learned the meaning of words like pyrolysis and anaerobic digestion, and is trying to persuade Donald MacDonald that these are the future. It's an uphill struggle. Donald is still something of a 'find a big hole and fill it in' kind of chap, and knows of some enormous chasms in Cloggley which he thinks would look better sort of smoothed out a bit.

Nicola is proud of having introduced a system where every report to Cabinet – on any subject – now incorporates an assessment of its Environmental Implications. This involves ticking one of four options:

- ❏ Very Positive
- ❏ Moderately Positive
- ❏ Marginally Positive
- ❏ Positively Marginal

This is completed by the authors of reports, who (working as they do in places like Adult Care or Catering, and unfettered by relevant expertise) are capable of highly interesting assessments. The Chief Executive has however drawn the line at a similar approach for Environmental Appraisals and Strategic Environmental Assessments: for a short period citizens were required to complete these whenever they had their bedrooms decorated or bought a nice new dining suite.

One unusual aspect of the Council's approach to green issues is its involvement in a number of Partnerships for Sustainability with communities in developing nations. These facilitate exchanges of ideas, materials and professional expertise aimed at developing a mutual understanding of planetary environmental issues.

The City's planners explain why, having messed up ourselves, we'd rather other countries didn't follow our example. They provide their opposite numbers with old plan chests and unused local plan policies; explain how they're making a positive contribution to solving the problems of rising sea levels in the Indian Ocean by joining in Bike To Work Day (and are slightly surprised at how well this latter initiative has taken off overseas); and show their hosts how to calculate permitted development rights and developer contributions. They offer advice on how to engage with amenity societies and other stakeholders. And they discuss differences between the Ombudsman and indigenous approaches to conflict resolution; without this it is unlikely that the City Council would now be seeing the benefits of voodoo applied to Planning for Real. The planners usually return home from visits with nice souvenirs carved from ivory, a warm glow of appreciation and an unfamiliar disease.[2]

Cloggley

If the City appears to be making considerable strides towards a thoroughly sustainable future, their neighbours to the east threaten to leave them standing. Cloggley has committed itself to an ambitious objective to become a net carbon-*consuming* Borough by 2012, although Peter Rabbit hasn't the faintest idea how this will be achieved.

Nothing less would be expected from a Council whose own residents have embraced the challenges posed by the threat of global warming with enthusiasm, urgency and extraordinary creativity. Spittle Jam Makers Against Climate Change have led the way in the field of sustainably managed conserves, Upper Gumtry residents are running their shared car on composted organic pak choi, and this year's WI calendar features 'Twelve Steps to Knit Your Own Water Butt'.

---

2 This joke has been recycled for environmental reasons.

The Council's officers have been impressed by the City's efforts to engage with overseas partners. They are not surprised to find that their colleagues from the developing world are better at this kind of thing than we are. Despite their lack of expertise in eco-auditing and modal shift, they seem to live less profligate lives. Peter Rabbit thinks there's a lesson in this but he's not quite sure what it is. Discussions over a Horlicks after his stamp collecting séances have been lively. Old Frank (speciality, Maltese greeny-blue 2d 1876–92) thinks that if we've had an industrial revolution they should be allowed to have one too. Audrey (the postal history of Wobberleigh between the Wars) disagrees and thinks they should restrain themselves so we can carry on using dishwashers. Winnie (anything with a cat on it) thinks we should go back to foraging and eat nettles. Arthur (anything with a train on it) wants to keep his car but is willing to walk as far as the shops. It is, thinks Peter, this independence of spirit which makes Cloggley the place it is.

Grimethwaite

The view of most Grimethwaite residents is 'why should we be botherin' 'bout t'bloody environment, it's done bugger all for us', and this approach is glumly endorsed by their elected representatives. Nonetheless the Council has recently, and after considerable and heated debate, resolved to opt into the global ecosystem.

It has however done little to further the objectives of environmental protection – though at least there is now a notice telling councillors not to leave the television in the Members' room on standby.

Let's Not Forget the Environment Agency

Other public authorities have been keen to develop sophisticated policies. The **Environment Agency**, for example, has consulted widely on a policy called 'managed realignment' of coastal defences in the north west which would, *inter alia*, involve more or less the whole of Grimethwaite becoming an active part of a naturally functioning flood plain. This option scored surprisingly highly on the cost benefit model used. Opportunities for the introduction of exotic flora and fauna, such as mangroves, mosquitoes and alligators, are exciting ecologists at the ~~Polytechnic~~ University (pending) and will add interest to any visit to the Colossus of Muckthorpe.

Conclusion

There can be little doubt that, as time goes by, as the waters of the Irish Sea begin to lap the shores of Muckthorpe and the fringes of the Sahara reach the plains of Cramshaw Superior, the environment will rise up the Grotton agenda, as surely, necessarily and essentially it should, must and will.

chapter nine

Management in Crisis

Organisational Structures Come and Organisational Structures Go[1]

As the world now knows, Grotton County Council has at last scored 'Average and with Moderate Prospects of Remaining Average' in the annual Comprehensive Area Assessment round. But it goes without saying that this impressive result was not achieved without massive, radical and, above all, frequent restructuring of the way the Council's services are provided, all of which are clearly essential if the continued commitment and energies of 'our most precious resource', the staff, were to be secured 'going forward'.

The material contained in this chapter has been prepared by *perpetualMotion LLP*, management consultants of Alderley Edge. Now in their third full year of practice, they are acknowledged leaders in the field of bespoke transformational re-baselining, having already restructured themselves four times without any loss of income. Recent clients include Barings Bank, Woolworth, Portsmouth FC and the Royal Town Planning Institute. Grotton County Council fully recognises the quality of *perpetualMotion*'s work: as Director of Transport and Environment Donald MacDonald has said, 'What those people at *perpetualMotion* keep coming up with is beyond belief.'

1 Rab C Nesbitt.

(facing) Dunromin's Chief Executive
likes to keep a low profile

Effecting Economy in Efficiency: The Grotton Experience

Signposts on a route map to excellence

Prepared by Senior Consultant Samantha Sloop

Executive Summary

A paradigm shift in comparative benchmarking has enabled Grotton authorities to disaggregate fluently. By pulling cross-cutting improvement levers and cascading via a pow-wow mechanism, the organisation has successfully ended in tiers. A holistic basket is in place to take structures to the next level.

Executive Summary Summarised

Progress evident, but further work required: our estimate is in the post.

Performance Management: The Business Plan

1. Our analysis of the management systems in place in **Grotton County Council** in 1979, which appear to have remained unchallenged for many years, revealed a primitive lack of baseline organisational techniques which would be regarded as critical to the running of any half-decent local authority today. Amazingly, they seemed nevertheless to be able to carry out a few basic functions, such as development planning and control (*sic*), building roads, and whatever else Metropolitan Counties did. Since then, the County Council has suffered under the burden of having to look after children and old people, running libraries and the like – no doubt worthy functions, but ones which can readily absorb funds unless very strict discipline is applied resource-management-wise.

2. The introduction of appropriately recalibrated systems to enhance holistic governance means that delivery of these 'coalface' functions has now been robustly downsized to reflect resource prioritisation; the resultant economies have enabled the County Council, with the essential involvement of *perpetualMotion*, to develop a range of fit-for-purpose back-office management systems that have reoriented the direction of travel, provided many new jobs within the corporate centre of the Authority, and significantly improved the range of out-of-office messages on the answerphone.

3. This crucial input was clearly key to the Authority's recent CAA ranking, and we at *perpetualMotion* are delighted that the Council have been able to share in our success.

4. At the heart of the County Council's approach lies the radical revision on an annual basis of the system of performance management or 'Business Plan', which is designed to cascade immutably from high level blue sky kite flying, via structured aspirational objective generation in the executive troposphere (with bonuses) to measurable targets at tea-lady level. Combined with effective disciplinary procedures at the middle and lower tiers, this will enhance teamwork in all areas and build commitment and loyalty to the organisation by ensuring staff are quite clear what they are meant to do – and what will happen to them if they don't.

5. Accordingly, in 2008, and following an intensive programme of in-house workshops and stakeholder focus groups, we were able to develop with the Authority a streamlined process cascading from an initial 'Philosophy': after considering a number of options including 'Grotton – We Got Big by Bothering' and 'Grotton: Angel of the North', the Council opted for 'Grotton – Serves You Right' – and this Philosophy lies very much at the heart of public service in the county.

6. From this Philosophy and its Core Values, the Corporate Management Team developed a bold 'Mission Statement': 'To make Grotton quite nice, all things being considered, or at least stop them getting much worse, and provided it doesn't cost us too much, what with inflation and everything'. Though we would have preferred something like 'Towards Excellence, Exceeding Better than the Very Best of the Very Best', *perpetualMotion* were nevertheless able to create from this Mission Statement an ambitious and lucrative Development Programme for the Council Plan, leading from a raw Vision, through Policy Steers, Service Plan Aims and Objectives, to Goals, Key Task Areas, and eventually individual SMART targets. See the diagram overleaf in case any of this is unclear.

The Chief Executive relaxes after a strenuous focus group meeting

Grotton County Council: The Business Planning Process – a simplified diagram

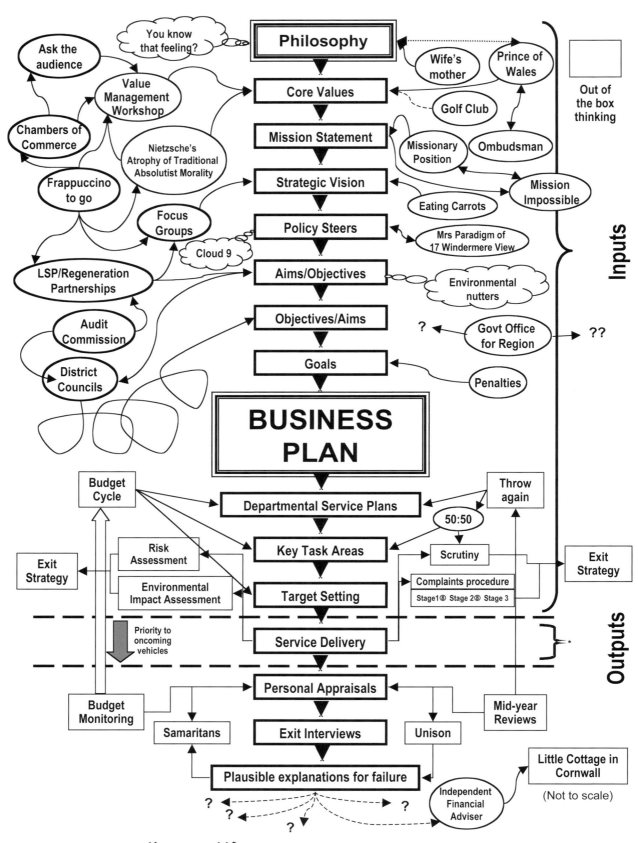

7. Although this is a three-year programme of envisioning work not due to be completed until 2011, the County Council has nevertheless taken the view that it will in the meantime continue to provide some limited services to stakeholders, or 'members of the public' as they are sometimes referred to.

8. In 2009, in the spirit of Continuing Challenge (our own company Mission Statement – for this year anyway – is 'If It Works, Fix It'), we have introduced a highly innovative bottom-up approach to performance management, having its heart in individual empowerment, its lungs in self-assessment and its spleen in the annual appraisal interview. As a result, the Council now derives its service plan SMART targets from individual officers' work programmes, leading via a seamless – one might almost say invisible – nylon thread through Key Task Areas, Goals, Objectives and Aims to Policy Steers, Vision, Mission Statement, Core Values and Philosophy, thus entirely reversing the previous approach, the clear benefits from which change seem almost too obvious to enumerate.

9. Council Leader Branston Pickles has emphasised the central role of the **Business Plan** in managing the performance of the Authority. As he told one of our Associate Directors over a highly goals-oriented buffet, 'I have come to appreciate, with your invaluable help, that there needs to be some sort of mechanism for demonstrating an improvement in services since we took over, as well as enabling us to put a positive spin on the many failings of our officers'.

10. Pickles has highlighted some of the key successes identified in the previous year's Transport and Environment section of the Business Plan, 'We were particularly proud to be recognised for the tendering process for the highly acclaimed cover of the Annex to our Waste and Minerals Annual Monitoring Report, and the speed of our "No comments" response to the Secretary of State's proposed changes to the Regional Spatial Strategy'.

Sustaining Local Democracy: The Committee Report

11. At the very heart, of course, of the local democratic process is **The Committee Report**.

12. In this area **Grotton City Council** has drawn extensively on the unparalleled expertise of *perpetualMotion*, brought to bear through a role-playing team development challenge model which we ran on a rewarding weekend on Helvellyn. (The great majority of the Authority's senior management have now, we are delighted to report, been located.)

13. The Chief Executive's extensive and growing team of Policy Co-ordinators and Policy Liaison Officers now oversees a comprehensive matrix management approach to ensuring that the implications of all decisions are thoroughly evaluated against a basket of local, regional, national and international policies, standards and imperatives. Or, to simplify, proposals are tested primarily, though obviously not entirely, through a meta-analysis in reports prepared for Committees and other stakeholder bodies of the possible synergy of every activity paradigm.

14. An illustration of the Council's current corporate report template, taken at random from a recent meeting of the Planning and Transport Committee, appears below:

Report to Planning Committee 18 June 2009

Title of Report:
Proposed change of use from Estate Agents to Mandelson's Fish and Chip Emporium and Budget Tanning Studio at no. 2 Victoria Parade, Grotton

Report of (Chief Officer):
N Tilbrook

Contact Officer:
Debbie Potter, Planning Assistant (extn 1722), but I may be on maternity leave by the time of the meeting

Purpose of Report, if any:
To consider a possible change of use and help members decide if they want to give it planning permission

Financial Implications:
None, I don't think

Human Rights Implications:
Human Rights Act doesn't apply to estate agents

Access to Information Implications:
Application file kept under my desk in Room 21 in the basement

Political Implications:
Grotton St Peters is a highly marginal seat

Disability Discrimination Act Implications:
Mr Mandelson's friend has a bad knee

Equal Opportunities Implications:
I've told you: Mr Mandelson's friend has a bad knee

Obesity Implications:
The applicant says he is fully behind Government policy on this: he will install narrow doors to prevent fat people getting in. Or out

Five a Day Monitoring Implications:
The mushy peas supplied will be free trade and from certificated organic suppliers

Climate Change Implications:

> The applicant is exploring the feasibility of recirculating extracted fat from the fryers to the tanning studio upstairs. And vice versa

Other Environmental Implications:

> The batter will be of local origin and derived from sustainably managed sources

Crime and Disorder Implications:

> The proposal will mean one fewer estate agent

Background Documents:

> Same as Access to Information box, I think

Consultations and Representations:

> Environmental Health say they have no objections, subject to a condition requiring there be separate storage of aloe vera and malt vinegar

> County Council's Highways Development Control say the development must comply with their normal standards for combined takeaways and tanning studios

> Seventeen letters of support for the proposal have been received, all welcoming the closure of the estate agents

> One letter of objection has been received from SIDS CHIPP'Y of no. 4 Victoria Parade, saying 'Everyone knows Mandelsons chips are smoother than ours because of the extra grease and we may go out of business'

Assessment:

> Policy S.27 of the Unitary Development Plan supports the closure of estate agents wherever feasible. I can't find any policies on combined takeaways and tanning studios. The possible loss of SIDS, while potentially a material consideration, is in my view outweighed by the broader benefits of the loss of estate agent related activity

Recommendation:

> Grant permission, subject to whatever the Highways man means

Reason for Recommendation:

> Policy S.27 of the Unitary Development Plan supports the closure of estate agents wherever feasible. I can't find any policies on combined takeaways and tanning studios. The possible loss of SIDS, while potentially a material consideration, is in my view outweighed by the broader benefits of the loss of estate agent related activity

Managing the Human Resource

15. *perpetualMotion* is delighted to have been of assistance in the **County Council**'s recent overhaul of what used to be termed personnel management practices.

16. Until our recent intervention the Council was slavishly following a sadly outmoded approach to **recruitment** by simply drawing up 'job descriptions' and 'person specifications' and evaluating 'applicants' against them in the hope of finding the 'best' candidate! With our help the Authority has now introduced a rather more sophisticated regime: various 'interviews', 'in-tray and role play exercises' and other evaluation methodologies are utilised, the outcomes carefully assessed and scored and, if the result seems likely to produce an unhelpful result, meticulously recalibrated to ensure the most suitable person emerges at the culmination of the process.

17. We have been able to bring to bear our particular expertise in the field of **senior management recruitment**.

18. *perpetualMotion* provided 'headhunting' services to the County Council in its search for a new Director of Human Capital. We were delighted to offer our own Co-ordinator of Competences, Knowledge and Aptitude, Rupert Abernethy, as a candidate and thrilled when he left us to join the Council.

19. A self-taught expert in psychometric testing, he was able to explain at his interview that he could not exactly say why he wanted the job, since Likert responses to questions needed to be summarised by the range across quartiles (or in certain circumstances by employing the standard deviation), or analysed using non-parametric methods such as the Chi-square, C-Beebie assigned rank or Barnes Wallis tests. He acknowledged that parametric analysis of ordinary median values of Seinfeld scale data could be justifiable by the Central Limit Theorem, but didn't know how that would help. Since all the interview panel had left by the time he had reached the end of his reply, and there were no other candidates for the job, he had been appointed by the cleaning lady.

20. Staff being the Council's key asset, as they are frequently told while having their increments frozen and training budgets cut, the Authority has in place a set of structured approaches to **induction** and **development**.

21. The introduction of a weekly **appraisal interview** for all staff now provides a welcome opportunity to test whether the 'aptitude for photocopying' identified in the job specification as an essential attribute really is in place, or whether a 'development need' can be identified and a structured, costed training plan put in place. An example of a typical output from this popular process appears opposite:

Appraiser's comments

Jonathan had a shaky start and his induction might, with benefit, have been extended to cover the identity and location of his work colleagues. Nevertheless he has worked well in his second year. He has enjoyed making the tea for his colleagues and the user satisfaction survey demonstrates a 70% approval rate. He has made a lot of new friends. His commitment to saving the planet does him great credit, and perhaps we should think about putting some distance between his workstation and Bernard's if his enthusiasm is to remain undimmed. The clerical error that has led to him being given four exit interviews was regrettable. Carry on the good work!

Personal Development Plan

2008–2009 Development opportunity identified: increased familiarity with planning legislation and framework: series of 12 interactive workshops identified in London

Achieved: one talk on Use Classes Order from Trevor Roberts Associates, plus two editions of Planning circulated

2009–2010 Development opportunity identified: to lead the Council's team at the High Court challenge to the Regional Spatial Strategy

22. With our help, the County Council has recently introduced a highly fit-for-purpose **attendance management** policy. Each and every visit paid by a member of staff to the kitchen, toilet or photocopier is now followed immediately by a 'return to work' interview with the Team Manager, who then compiles a report indicating reasons for absence and the raft of measures agreed to facilitate a re-induction to the workplace, phased if necessary. Both manager and employee are supported throughout this process.

23. The protocols requiring line managers to visit staff who are away from the office on long-term sick leave have recently been updated following a number of ill-advised (and, in one case, sadly fatal) attempts to interview employees while in intensive care.

24. **Retention** of staff at the County Council appears to present a similar challenge to that experienced by other authorities around the country: once in post they tend to stay. A good deal of information is gleaned from **exit interviews** and recorded on file in case anyone can think of a use for it.

Customer Focus in Dunromin

25.   *perpetualMotion* is the first to recognise that we are not the only consultancy with expertise in this important field. The Royal Borough of Dunromin, for reasons of their own, recently elected not to invite us to assist in refocusing their efforts to bring a sharper customer orientation to service delivery, but to retain instead the distinctive services of A2Zee, worthy competitors of ours in the field of managing client expectation strategies. We have been able to obtain examples of their work for Dunromin, and can unreservedly commend A2Zee for their apparent expertise in certain areas. We are confident the Council will have detected benefits in some of their findings and recommendations.

26.   In particular, we note that a major departmental restructuring has taken place each year since 1992, following A2Zee's advice, and twice a year over the past decade. The current Corporate Management Team, as at 3 October 2009, comprises:

- Chief Executive
- Deputy Chief Executive and Head of Policy, Performance Management, Equalities Monitoring, Human Resources and Communications
- Director of Scrutiny (frozen post)
- Director of Restructuring
- Director of Corporate, Democratic and Legal Services
- Director of Customer Focus (Promotion of Complaints)
- Director of Customer Focus (Investigation of Complaints)
- Director of Customer Focus (Blame Avoidance and Counselling)
- Director of Ombudsman Case Management
- Head of Actual Services (observer status)

27.   At the time of writing – and this is a very fluid area – we understand that the Chief Executive has wisely suggested to A2Zee that this structure may not be sufficiently customer focused, feeling that there needs to be a complete separation between the roles *inter alia* of complaint promotion, complaint recording, complaint investigation, complaint feedback and complaints against the other complaints divisions.

We include opposite, by way of illustration, a recent example of Dunromin's current Complaints Procedure in operation:

Name of complainant:
Norbert ('Nobby') Harbringer-Grudge RN OBE

Department:
☑ Planning ☐ Other Tick as appropriate

Nature of complaint:
Proposed development of house by Mr Belcher near Cramshaw Superior would be detrimental to the enjoyment of the dwelling house (viz. 'Beau Rivage') as such, due to overlooking and loss of privacy. He and Mrs H-G, with a number of close friends, occasionally practise the entirely healthy and innocent activity of 'nudism', and strongly object to the possibility of being seen without their clothes on. Also, that Ms Turpentine did not pay a visit to view the Rear Admiral's property.

Desired outcome:
Refusal of planning permission for proposed development and castration of relevant official for dereliction of duty.[2]

Stage 1
<u>Comment from Ms Turpentine</u>: Ms Turpentine did in fact very cautiously view the garden of Beau Rivage from the application site. Thankfully for all concerned, any possible sighting of the complainant, clothed or otherwise, was impossible due to the intervention of a dense belt of trees.

<u>Report of Investigating Officer</u>: Planning permission was refused some time ago. Therefore I find the complaint to be *nem con* and *post hoc*.

Stage 2
The Rear Admiral continues to argue that heads must be flogged and demands a visit from the Chief Executive in person to view the site of the nudist activities.

<u>Comment from the Chief Executive</u>: Ch Exec does not normally visit people who comment on planning applications, especially nudists, as he has other responsibilities, such as running the council.

Stage 3
<u>Report of Complaints Panel</u>: The Rear Admiral is a regular customer of the Panel and it is always nice to hear from him. The Panel was aware of his proclivities in the nudism department. We can all understand why the Rear Admiral (and especially his wife) should be placed on display only in private. However, the planning application of which he complained has been refused by the Royal Borough. We therefore rule that element of his complaint to be invalid due to supersedation. We do not believe that further action is required.

Omdudsman report:
Awaited

2 The Rear Admiral is short-sighted.

28. Although A2Zee have quite properly advised that this complaints-handling work can only be fully developed within a private sector environment, we have learned that the Council currently envisages it being accommodated entirely in-house – believed to be in part a belated response to their controversial, and ultimately unsuccessful, outsourcing in the 1990s of a management contract for fault reporting and complaints to Arnolfini Brothers of Sicily who took an exceptionally vigorous approach to the task, necessitating an early termination of the contract. The Council was able to use this experience as a learning opportunity – with the exception of the Head of Procurement, which was found on the Chief Executive's pillow.

29. A2Zee have also carried out a superficial analysis of the complaints themselves and found the performance of the public in this respect to be of a frequently poor standard. They classified many complaints (as well as members of the public) as being badly presented, ill-informed and wholly irrational. This is something *perpetualMotion* could have told them years ago.

30. With or without the well-intentioned input provided by A2Zee, Dunromin can take a good deal of satisfaction from its increased focus on this vital aspect of its work. The Authority's energetic efforts to promote its complaints procedure are bearing fruit and the Council now receives 200% more complaints about its services than in 2004, requiring it to deploy several dozen more staff in the process; this in turn has meant a reduction in staffing levels in frontline services, which of course has led to a further increase in complaints, and there is no reason why this process should not continue.

31. The ultimate test is how speedily (but not necessarily how successfully) the Authority responds to complaints about its complaints procedure; this is something which A2Zee unaccountably ignored in their otherwise entirely reasonably decent piece of work. The Council know where to come if they wish to move forward in this specialist field.

Tomorrow's Future Starts Today

32. With *perpetualMotion*'s unique input, the Grotton authorities are now, management-wise, where Halifax hoped to be yesterday and where Rochdale would have wished to have been the day after that. And there's no reason to believe that, with the continuing commitment of all concerned, we shouldn't be able to look forward to a long-term, lucrative and ultimately pointless collaboration.

33. It has been an honour for *perpetualMotion* to be able to share our vision with all the thousands of potential clients who we hope will be reading this book. Please visit our stand in the Titanic Suite.

The Grotton Advertiser

Established 1888. Incorporating the Bletherley Sentinel. No. 6015

IN PRAISE OF ... PLANNERS

HAVE YOU NOTICED that town planners seem to be everywhere at the moment? You can't move for them, as they gather on street corners to gaze admiringly at Grotton's Victorian heritage, or just hang out in one of Bletherley's inviting wine bars. There's no escape – on another page, one of our readers reports how she found one in her airing cupboard and had to shoo it away with a brush.

But we can reveal that it's no accident that The Planners are in Town. For this week, the eyes of the world will be on Greater Grotton, as literally lots of delegates – some from as far afield as Doncaster and Didcot Parkway – come together to mark the 31st anniversary of the last time something similar happened.

Planning is never far from the news. Week after week, our pages are filled with heart-rending stories of old ladies being told by Council officials to demolish their conservatories with their bare hands, and motorists having to drive round in circles for weeks at a time trying to get mobile phone coverage.

So today, the *Advertiser* asks 'are planners any use?' And the answer may surprise some readers – on balance, we say 'yes, mostly'.

We admit that, over the years, we have been critical of them in these columns. But that is the role of a responsible press – to scrutinise, to hold to account. Why, for example, do our planners still make it almost impossible to turn right at the Back

Vatican Street roundabout? Why do they keep demolishing much-loved local pubs and post offices? And why, despite our campaign, do they continue to resist calls to revise the methodology underpinning the local development framework's environmental impact assessments?

So, as the last of the bunting is strung across the venerable face of the St Vitus Centre, and extra supplies of Raggett's Rustic Implausible are front-loaded from Muckthorpe's famous brewery, we say to Britain's planners: 'Welcome for a bit. May wisdom and hard work govern your deliberations. May the weather be kind, the locals friendly and the food edible.'

And spend, spend, spend.

Cloggley: 'Free-Fire Zone For Planning Cowboys' – MP

By staff reporter TONY FYSON, standing pointlessly outside the Civic Centre

'HOW ON EARTH did *that* get planning permission?' That's the question we all ask whenever we drive past Bletherley Civic Centre.

For the answers, I went to see Peter Rabbit. In the planning business longer than all the other Council bosses put together, Rabbit should know a thing or two. And what he told me came as a bit of a shock. 'Well, it might come as a bit of a shock, Tony,' he said, 'but loads of things can happen out there which don't actually need planning permission.'

I asked him how come.

Complicated

Well, planning rules are pretty complicated. For example, he told me that, thanks to some bureaucratic sleight-of-hand called the 'Useless Class Order', your local butchers can shut up on a Saturday and reopen Monday morning as an 'adult' bookshop.

Without the Council's say-so.

But if he tries to sell hot Cornish pasties, he's likely to get a visit from an 'enforcement officer'. Incredibly, this unelected functionary can confiscate the pasties and have the building demolished.

Rabbit agreed that this was the sort of thing the public would have difficulty understanding. Especially if the pasties were any good.

It's amazing what some people get up to, particularly if they know their way through planning's many loopholes. Rabbit showed me some examples. A scrap-metal dealer who claimed nocturnal panel beating was a lifelong hobby and was something called 'permitted development'. An operator of a not-allowed open-cast coal mine in his back garden who couldn't see anything wrong. He told Radio Chirpy 'by the time I've finished, the site will look exactly as it did before – it'll just be the other way up'.

Gripe

A common gripe by Cloggley's hard-pressed councillors is the number of people who apply to do things they've already done without asking. Planners' jargon for this is 'retrospective' applications.

One I spoke to, who didn't want to be named, told me 'It's absolutely outrageous. In my book, anyone who builds something without getting planning permission first should be

CLOGGLEY'S PLANNERS are still struggling to understand the permitted development regime

reported to the police, placed on the sexual offenders' register and then shot'. Others seemed to take a more tolerant line. Cllr Audrey Bullocks (Con: Blether Valley) is typical. 'I think it's only fair to give people a friendly warning before reporting them to the police. But I agree wholeheartedly that they should eventually be shot.'

CLOGGLEY MEADOWS – just one of the hundreds of enforcement cases the Council has to tackle every year

Cutting Edge: The Village Barber is now open on Tuesdays

Mast *'Death Ray'* fear

From our special correspondent A R G FYSON, standing pointlessly in a field near Upton-on-t'Bogg

Advertiser exclusive!

IF THERE'S ONE issue that gets people out on the streets it's mobile phone masts. Just look what happened to the application for a mast in a field near Upton-on-t'Bogg. Local resident Phyllida Bean said 'there's a school not 1500 metres from the site. Since we first found out about it, there's been unexplained outbreaks of eczema, double vision, runny noses, all kinds of things. Heaven knows what will happen if it actually gets built'.

Dunromin has more than its fair share of these masts. I asked the local MP Digby Struthers for a comment. 'It's time for common sense,' he explained. 'Enough is enough. At the end of the day, as I have pointed out on many occasions, it's a matter of balance. The planners simply need to get a grip.'

Fears

Struthers was less coherent when it came to his constituents' fears about the impact of masts on public health. 'I've been on the internet, and it's quite clear that our children will quite simply fry to death. This could interfere with their education. Who would you rather believe – bureaucrats and boffins or the people who actually have to live within sight of these things? Vote Struthers – the man who generally agrees with you.'

The *Advertiser* tried to contact Vodafone for a comment, but we couldn't get a signal.

POLY PUZZLE SHOCK HORROR

From our planning and cookery correspondent Anthony J P Fyson standing pointlessly outside the ~~Polytechnic~~ University (pending)

SOME OF THE issues planners have to deal with are really quite complicated. In this major feature our specialist reporter Anthony Fyson tells how the big decisions are made.

Due to an oversight, plans dating from 1986 to turn the Poly into a University are still 'pending'. But it's only a matter of time.

One of the things which Universities have to have is snazzy new buildings. In 1999 planners at Grotton City Council were hit with a scheme for a new block in St Anne's Passage to house the Department of Obverse Biometrics and Interpretative Media Postulation.

Outrage

Outrage followed when the *Advertiser* first reported on the modernist plan for a massive flat-roofed red and blue ceramic tower block, five storeys high, to replace the much loved Old Building (see above) – well known as the place where custard was first synthesised. 'It's a scandal,' said the Friends of the Old Building. 'It's an affront,' said Lieut-Col Harbringer-Grudge, of Bletherley. 'It's an abomination,' said the Grotton Preservation Society, describing the scheme as 'massive and overbearing' and 'out of keeping with its surroundings'.

Blob

'No one has taken the slightest bit of notice of this nondescript edifice for over eighty years' said architect Caligula Spruce at the time. As the designer of the new building dubbed by locals 'the blob', he was 'miffed' that suddenly preserving a '… uniquely boring building …' had become a *cause célèbre*.

'The University (pending) needs to make a statement' said Spruce. 'It needs to say "We are here, we are modern, we have a dream". And it needs to say it in red and blue ceramics at least five storeys high.' And, he added, routinely, 'Just look at Bilbao.'

Experts are divided. English Heritage have described the Old Building as 'not without merit, and having obvious historical curiosity' and have listed the façade and the famous 'Custard Room'.

'Rubbish'

Government advisers CABE, however, have described the Old Building as a 'heap of old rubbish' and strongly support the Spruce scheme. 'This low rise building will be constructed largely of local brick with some minor ceramic decoration,' they point out. 'Arguments that it is overbearing are exaggerated. This view is based on the fact that it is the same height as surrounding buildings. As to whether it fits in with the general ambience, it must be said that – being designed by an architect of some skill and imagination – it does not. However it would be wrong to penalise the University (pending) for employing a half-decent architect.'

St Anne's Passage is in some need of refurbishment, and CABE have welcomed a plan to tidy up the entrance and improve the landscaping.

Rage

The saga continues. Members of the Grotton Preservation Society yesterday marched to the Town Hall to present a petition. Peaceful at first, the scene turned ugly later in the day, with police having to deny allegations that Lieut-Col Harbringer-Grudge's injuries were caused by them. 'He attacked my truncheon with his head,' Constable Puffin told reporters.

In an exclusive interview, planning boss Nicola Tilbrook told me 'the proposal seems to be in line with all the policies in the Grotton City Council Local Plan, Design Guide, and Development Control Policy Statement'.

'Monstrosity'

The *Advertiser* put this to Lieut-Col Harbringer-Grudge. 'There is a petition of over 357 signatures against this monstrosity,' he said, 'with not a single vote in favour. Surely that means that they have to turn it down. That's what democracy is all about. It's all very well for them to blind us with science. We demand satisfaction.'

The outcome remains to be seen. But what will the planners at the conference make of it? Are the organisers embarrassed that this row is going on just as delegates arrive? 'No,' said Koffi Break, incredibly. 'This kind of thing happens all the time. Delegates will be quite used to it.'

+++ *Briefs* +++

Planners have to do many different things. The Advertiser's team of reporters outline some of the recent controversies which have hit the headlines here in Greater Grotton

Local Business Group Welcomes Supermarket Giant

By staff reporter T J Fyson standing pointlessly next to the bypass

Bletherley Chamber of Commerce Chairman Malcolm Stoat today welcomed the news that Tesco are planning to open a new superstore in the town.

'We very much welcome this news,' says Malcolm, 53. 'It's just what Bletherley needs. It will be very convenient for all our shopping needs, and create plenty of new jobs.'

Local Business Group Hits Out At Loss of Small Shops

By staff reporter J T Fyson standing pointlessly in Prince Regent Avenue, Bletherley

Bletherley Chamber of Commerce Chairman Malcolm Stoat today slammed news of a continuing reduction in the number and variety of small shops in the town, according to its annual membership survey, published today.

'The decline in Bletherley's small independents is a continuing concern,' says Malcolm, 54. 'They are the lifeblood of the town and jobs are being lost all the time. We will be pressing the Council for action.'

Grotton Book 'Out of Date'

By our Literary Correspondent Ant Fyson standing pointlessly outside Routledge HQ

Authors of a new book about Grotton have admitted that it is out of date. A spokesperson said 'The election is very inconvenient for a lot of people. And they keep mucking about with the planning rules anyway. Unless it was printed before we'd finished, we were bound to be in dead trouble up-to-dateness wise. We just hope our readers will understand.'

The Royal Town Planning Institute sought to distance itself, saying that it would be having a close look at the authors' CPD records.

The book, the first to be written about Grotton since the authors' own *Grotton Papers* (1979), lifts the lid on planning in the County and is said to be 'very funny'.

'Chopping Copses Cheaper than Bashing Cops' – Claim

From our tree correspondent A C 'Stumpy' Fyson, standing pointlessly under a tree

Green groups from all over the County were up in arms today after local builder Brendan O'Reilly (not a stereotype) was fined a 'pathetic' £15 for taking a chain saw to a group of 200-year-old beech trees on his land at Cholmondley Park. 'You get done for more than that just for thumping a copper' said 'Squidgy' (not his real name) of local campaign group Barking Mad.

Magistrates heard that O'Reilly, 46, admitted 'accidentally' felling over forty of the protected trees in less than ten minutes. He denied that his actions had anything to do with his long-standing attempts to develop the land for housing. Speaking through his solicitor, O'Reilly claimed he had intended to carry out some light seasonal pruning. He had suffered a 'momentary lapse of concentration' while checking the racing results on his mobile phone. Failing that, his eyesight wasn't as good as it used to be. And anyway he had always given generously to the local scout troop.

Grotton stipendiary magistrate Rear Admiral Norbert (Nobby) Harbringer-Grudge is 89.

War Hero in House Extension Refusal Shock

From our war correspondent Capt T 'Tubby' Fyson

Local MP Digby Struthers today branded Dunromin's planners 'heartless and unpatriotic'. After a 2½ hour debate, the Council's so-called Development Management and Continuous Performance Improvement Panel voted to kick out an application by 84-year-old George Gormley to allow him to keep a PVCu lean-to he has built at his neat semi in Gladstone Gardens, Bletherley. Gormley was said to be 'gobsmacked' by the decision.

Council heritage officer, Jason Beetling (18), told the *Advertiser*: 'We made it clear to Mr Gormley that PVCu was inappropriate in a conservation area. The lean-to should be demolished and rebuilt with fair-trade recycled mahogany from a sustainable, and preferably local, source. This would respect the traditional design details, or what we call the vernacular, at the same time as saving the planet.'

Struthers said: 'This is bureaucracy run mad. The man's a national hero. If I had my way, the planners would be strung up by their vernaculars.'

Mr Gormley, who sprained his ankle quite badly at the Battle of Arnhem, told reporters: 'Right, that's it. If that's the way they're going to treat me, I'll never fight for my country again.'

Even more Briefs on the next page!

Parking row sparks resident's anger

From our motoring correspondent A J 'Jeremy' Fyson

'How do they think I'm going to manage?' That was the reaction of local resident Diane von Furstenburg when Cloggley planners told her she could not concrete over her front garden. 'I've got five teenagers and they've all got a car plus the 4x4 and my hubby's car and my little runabout,' she explained. 'I need at least ten spaces allowing for when my friends come round. Where else are they supposed to park?'

Planning supremo Peter Rabbit said he was not very keen on paving over gardens as it didn't look very nice. 'Rather a rose than a Renault,' he quipped. 'And also Upton-on-t'Bogg might get flooded.'

'Democracy denied' Council Leader says

From our undercover reporter 'Fyson' standing pointlessly in a pub

Tempers boiled over in Bletherley this morning. A Planning Inspector has allowed an application for a wind farm to be built in Wobberleigh. Council Leader Sir Hartley Hartley-Wintergrene said 'This is a nightmarish attempt by a discredited Labour Government to ride roughshod over public opinion. It's centralisation gone mad, a Stalinist project to bypass local democratic institutions, like the poll tax farrago which all right we brought in but it was a good idea at the time, who's this person from Bristol to tell us what to do?'

The single turbine wind farm will be forty feet high.

NEWS OF THE wind farm has raised eyebrows locally

YESSS!!!! Local Businessman Ollie Burke celebrates the updated windfall assumptions in the Regional Spatial Strategy

Letters to the Editor

Sir
My enjoyment of *Grotton Revisited* was entirely spoiled by its inaccuracy. Don't the authors know that the term 'average' has never been used? Grotton was of course 'weak' – a big improvement on 'poor'; then it got a star; now it's 'an organisation that meets only minimum requirements'. Surely this is simple enough? Get a grip!
Winifred Molyneux
Audit Commission

Sir
Grotton Revisited is riven with inaccuracy. In particular my own entirely constructive role in fashioning the future of Grotton from a swatch of unpromising material is irremediably underplayed.

The Department's lawyers are examining the issue and should have a response by the end of next year.
Alexander Quibble CB
Government Office

Dear Sir
I just thought I'd like to say what a nice book *Grotton Revisited* is. Jolly well done to all concerned.
P Rabbit
Cloggley

Sir
For F Drains's information, the Lancashire Fusiliers did not reach the Battle of the Limpopo until 2.15 on the third day.
Branston Pickles
Sleightley

PLANNING: *YOUR QUESTIONS ANSWERED*

What's on your mind?

Note: The *Advertiser* is not responsible for the accuracy of any of the information contained in this (or any other) feature

What are planners for?
Planners believe that the world can be improved by writing what they call policies, displaying them on coloured maps and asking other people to carry them out.

Does that work?
By and large, no.

But why are so many of them here in Grotton?
They have often met here before, most recently in 1979, and it doesn't seem to have done much harm. And local pubs did well out of it. Also, it's a lot cheaper than Bournemouth.

Didn't Mrs Thatcher abolish planning?
Not at all. There were some amusing misunderstandings at first, but all political parties now fully appreciate and support the role of planning in making the world a better place, say planners.

Why do planners always get things wrong?
They don't. The way the 'planning system' actually works means that mistakes are always being made

by people like architects, builders, engineers, councillors, civil servants, planners 'on the other side', and the public in general.

Can I opt out if I don't want any planning done, and get a rebate on my Council Tax?
Sadly, no. Even people living in places with little or no planning, like Grimethwaite, still have to pay Council Tax.

Is it easy to become a planner?
No. You've got to know a bit about geography, statistics, sociology, architecture, engineering, the law, cookery, management, public relations, finance, and much, much more, but not too much about any one of them. Getting the balance right is really, really hard.

Are there any famous planners?
Dennis Bergkamp's younger brother nearly accepted a place at university to study planning.

Will planners be a nuisance around the town?
Police advise that they will generally keep themselves to themselves if

not disturbed, but they may become agitated if they hear words like subsidiarity, or last orders, or Daily Mail. If you feel threatened, throw them a bit of jargon or an old bureaucrat.

How will I be able to recognise one?
There's no foolproof method. They can be of either sex (and some of the more flamboyant conservation experts might actually be both) and of virtually any age. Most will deny being planners if asked directly. You could hang around next to a couple of likely suspects deep in conversation – but if you're bored rigid after two minutes, they're likely to be chartered surveyors.

Will they be able to help me if I have a planning problem?
Yes! Planners are always happy to be rung in the evening or at the weekend with requests for information or to be given feedback on their performance. They call this 'community engagement'.

They shall not pass: Wobberleigh Parish Councillors are against any form of development

Boy Tory's Planning Story

By our Political Correspondent Nick Fyson

Dunromin schoolboy Jamie Balliol was relaxing at home today after writing the Conservative Party's policies on planning.

Balliol, 13, wrote the policies as a school essay project. But Headmaster Charles Winchester, of King William's School, Bletherley, was so impressed he sent them off to Party HQ. It seems the Tories liked them. They'd always said they were going to change the planning system (though they weren't sure why), and published the essay as a Green Paper earlier this year.

Though the paper was greeted with a storm of criticism, Balliol was unworried. He told me exclusively that he "knew nothing about planning really", but he'd tweeted his mates and "they'd come up with some awesome ideas 'n' stuff". His girlfriend, Lady Margaret Hall, had suggested the bit about third party appeals as Daddy had wanted to "beat the pen-pushers at their own game" after they gave permission for a house less than a mile from the family seat.

Balliol, who would like to be an MP if he grows up, thought the IPC had "had its day", and wanted to know where he could download Kasabian's latest album for free.

Developers bothering you?

YOU NEED A NEWT!

Even just one great crested newt is enough to stop the most ruthless developer in his tracks

Now you can get them discreetly delivered to your site, just in time for the Inspector's visit, from: Newts for Nimbies, Drake Farm, Cloggley www.newtsfornimbies.co.uk

Around Town

No. 1 for Showbiz!

By our Showbiz Correspondent Tara Palmer-Fyson

Was that *Sienna Miller* looking more than a little emotional in Grimethwaite today? A small crowd gathered as she opened the new Oxfam shop which has brought hope to the High Street in Muckthorpe. Wearing a low cut cerise jumpsuit which revealed her slim figure to perfection, she cut the ribbon and said "Thank God for the sequential test", before buying a couple of old paperbacks and some lego ("*pieces may not all be present*") and leaving rather hastily.

Rumours of a romance between *Miller* and Grimethwaite Planning supremo *Wayne Blunt*, have been denied by Council sources. Blunt, spotted looking "absolutely landscaped" leaving Cloggley's trendy "Squashed Banana" Club in the early hours, is said by friends to be "besotted".

And who was the mystery man snapped with fashion guru *Gok Wan* while mastering the intricacies of Grotton's decriminalised parking enforcement? "Demand management is so hot right now, so on-trend" says the bespectacled beguiler. He sooo didn't see that penalty charge notice coming! CRINGE!!!

Penelope Keith, who will be appearing in Dick Whittington this winter at the Theatre Royal, visited Grotton today. It was her first visit to the town. *Keith*, in a lime green twinset with matching shoes and handbag, said "What this place needs is a Core Strategy", before lunching at Mandelson's Fish Bar.

Melvyn Bragg passed through the Grotton area today on his way to Aylesbury.

Ports Policy "Pointless"

By our Maritime correspondent "Jolly Jack" Fyson

Grimethwaite Council Leader Sid Spriggs has slammed the Government's National Policy Statement on Ports.

"This is exactly what I expected. As usual it assumes ports have to be on the coast" said Spriggs. "We weren't even consulted about it. It's another example of the lack of vision at the top – looking for the easy way out. Just because widening the Blether Navigation needs a bit of effort! The Government should not be so namby-pamby. It should be prepared to think outside the box, whatever that means".

I asked Spriggs whether he agreed with the policy that port development should be left to market forces. "What are those?" he said. "We don't have them in Grimethwaite. This puts us at a disadvantage yet again". Spriggs thought that, as a planning document, the policy should include a bit of planning – a view described by Alexander Quibble of the Government Office as "naïve".

Appendices

Notes For Delegates

PLANNING IN CRISIS

~~Polytechnic~~ University (pending) of Central Grotton

5–9 September 2010

A conference to celebrate the achievement of Grotton County Council in attaining 'average' status in the Comprehensive Area Assessment

Also to mark the 31st Anniversary of the great 'Planning in Crisis' Conference at the Polytechnic of Central Grotton, 5–9 September 1979

Also to discuss the state of planning in these troubled times what with global warming, the collapsing economy, and the demise of old certainties, and the fact that none of us is getting any younger

TRANSPORT

By rail

The nearest station still open is Grotton Sludge Street. It is best to treat the information displayed on Platform 1 with some caution. Conference officials will be on hand, weather permitting, to tell delegates where to get off.

By road

It is conference policy for delegates to use public transport, but we realise nobody will take any notice.

From the Spittle i' th' Bottom interchange on the Grotton Ring Road, the best thing is to use the A9497, the B3549, then turn left onto the B2659, past where the Methodist Chapel used to be, then ask. Satnav is not yet operational in the Grotton area due to a black hole in the ether.

By air

The Ryan Giggs International Airport remains closed. In any event, delegates are strongly advised against travelling to Grotton by air, except possibly from Belgium.

ACCOMMODATION

Delegates will be accommodated in the luxurious Enron Hall of Residence in Ivy Lane, Wobberleigh, which is only three miles from the ~~Polytechnic~~ University (pending). Hot and cold running water mornings and some evenings; no rucksacks; please make bed. This was a PFI project; please take care – falling debris.

Meals will be taken in the Winter Gardens, Gas Street. Please replace trays on racks. Coffee extra. (NB The Winter Gardens is a Grade II Listed Building owned by the Council. Please avoid areas marked 'Keep out – Dry Rot'. Delegates with disabilities may prefer to eat elsewhere.)

CONFERENCE SESSIONS

Repairs to the Gordon Brown Lecture Theatre should be completed in time for the conference. Please arrive early to be sure of a bench.

Medical

If you feel unwell there is not much we can do about it. There is an NHS drop-in centre on Quartermain Avenue, next to the newsagents.

Health and Safety

There are doors at each exit point and our advice is that if there's a fire you should run like buggery.

Dr Öpik of the Department of Astrophysics at the ~~Polytechnic~~ University (pending) has warned that there is an imminent danger of a meteorite striking Grotton. Please wear a hard hat.

The conference organisers take no responsibility for the death or injury of any delegate however caused.

Telephones

There used to be a phone box by the bus station.

Church Services

Grotton Cathedral, Commercial Street (Anglican); Church of St Étienne, Back Vatican Street, Bletherley (RC); St Vitus United Primitive Evangelical Tabernacle, Cloggley.

Sports and Leisure

There is a leisure centre in Bletherley, with tennis, croquet and boules (members only); and there is still a swimming pool in Grimethwaite (now declared fairly safe by Environmental Health).

Badges

Badges MUST be worn at all times. There is a very good reason for this.

Publications

The following publications are available from the Conference Office:

Title	Extent	Price
History of Grotton	pp 26	£ 1.25
The problems of Grotton	pp 1999	£17.99
This Cloggley	pp 12	60p
What to do in an air raid	pp 3	2 ½ d
Dunromin Core Strategy – why it isn't ready (7th edn)	t.b.c	(gratis)
"A Wobberleigh WAG Looks Back" by Ludmilla Prosaič	pp 199	£19.99
Cartesian Entropy – Temporary Disequilibrium and the Night Time Economy – the Muckthorpe Exemplar by Deirdre Sulkie	pp 632	£245.47
Mildred Avenue and the Bauhaus – from Weimar to Grotton	pp 72	£1.45
A Life in Tarmac by Donald MacDonald	pp 243	£17.99
"Rubbish Revisited" – a Guide to Muckthorpe's World of Waste	pp 3	25p

Note: a list of delegates attending the conference is included in the conference papers. Selected telephone numbers and email addresses are available from the bookshop **for a fee**.

CONFERENCE PROGRAMME

DAY 1

10.00–11.00	National Policy Statements – why they have failed
11.00–12.00	Coffee
12.00–12.15	Discussion
12.15–2.30	Lunch

(AFTERNOON FREE)

6.30–9.00	Dinner
9.00–9.30	Ministerial Address (tbc*)

DAY 2

10.00–11.00	Local Development Frameworks – what's the point?
11.00–2.30	As Day 1

(AFTERNOON TOURS)

A	Cloggley's Shrinking Glaciers
B	Historic Grimethwaite (as per 1979 programme)
C	Unknown Bletherley

6.30–9.00	Dinner
9.00–9.30	Development Management - where we went wrong

DAY 3

10.00–11.00	Global Warming – are shorter committee reports really the answer?
11.00–2.30	As Day 1

(AFTERNOON FREE)

6.30–9.00	Dinner
9.00–9.30	The Recession – were the planners to blame?

DAY 4

10.00–11.00	Bottom Up or Top Down – can we have it both ways?
11.00–2.30	As Day 1

2.30–3.30	Life – is it worth living?
3.30	Conference ends

* to be confirmed or to be cancelled (to be confirmed)

EXHIBITION

The exhibition in the Central Vestibule will include displays by:

- CLG – display of motherhood and apple pie (organic)
- Muckthorpe Bottoms Urban Development Corporation will host a champagne reception at which they will unveil a model of the proposed Colossus (after the 9.00 watershed)
- Dunromin BC – display of award-winning staff appraisal forms
- A discretion-fettering demonstration will take place, led by Charles Silke QC

WORKSHOPS

A number of ancillary workshops will be held on the conference fringe.

1. The Environment Agency will be demonstrating how to get away with responding to consultations well after the deadline.
2. The CPRE will introduce their latest pamphlet 'Planning Applications we didn't object to, 1929–2008' (3 pp, 3 p).
3. The RIBA will explain why it supports the planning system, except when it doesn't.
4. *perpetualMotion* Management Consultants will be sponsoring a workshop on the role of gibberish in local government management.
5. Mrs Paradigm, of Windermere View, Muckthorpe, will explain why it would be nice if there were more things for young people to do.

FRINGE MEETING

Probity in Planning: What's in it for me?

The Freedom of Information Act 2000 resulted in a complete rewrite of Grotton City Council's Planning Code of Conduct. Up to that point, it had simply required members of the Development Control Committee to act in accordance with four Guiding Principles: Honesty, Accountability, Openness and above all, Nothing in Writing. This potentially explosive fringe meeting (speakers to be announced) asks whether the probity pendulum has swung too far.

WHO WILL BE PRESENT?

The Prince of Wales has been invited to speak on the subject of '*Why one considers oneself entirely justified in criticising schemes by Lord Rogers, yet why one feels it's better to do it behind the scenes, as it were*'. Should he attend, architects and *Guardian* readers will be excluded from the Conference. It may be necessary to exclude other delegates too, on the advice of the Grotton and Cloggley Constabulary, unless they have up-to-date biometric blood samples, iris recognition modules, a recent photograph with a gloomy expression, a Council Tax or Utilities bill, and a Union Jack.

We thought about inviting a Minister; we know they're ten a penny these days but we've tried anyway and we'll see whether he or she turns up.

The President of the RTPI will be present, whoever it is, and has been asked to wear a chain to aid recognition. Do not confuse with the Mayor of Grotton (93).

WHERE TO GO AND WHAT TO DO DURING CONFERENCE WEEK

Attractions

ACKROYD HALL, FOLLICLE ST, CLOGGLEY
No 36 bus every 2 hours
A Georgian House built for Jedediah Ackroyd in 1865, the Hall (now run by Cloggley Parks & Cemeteries Dept) contains a varied selection of paintings and artefacts assembled by successive Ackroyds during their travels. (NB Certain works acquired by Sir Benjamin when he was Viceroy of Hyderabad may be viewed by serious students only, on written application to the Curator).

GRIMETHWAITE MUSEUM OF MINING
Station Yard, Grimethwaite
(Closed until further notice due to subsidence.)

Parks and Gardens

GRIME VALLEY COUNTRY PARK
Temporarily landscaped slag heap off Muckthorpe Road. Orchids. Motorcyclists. Slag.

CARBUNCLE HALL OFFICE PARK, BLETHERLEY
Interesting examples of mid twentieth century office blocks. Valuable period extractor fans.

Entertainment

THE GROTTON SINFONIA
Cond Hans Pfütling
Victoria Park, 6 Sept
The Dream of Gerontius. Indoors if wet.

THE AD NAUSEAM ENSEMBLE
This innovative ensemble will perform a specially composed work for oboe, guitar and chanterelle, influenced by native Sierra Leone Tempura music and funk-driven Coulis from the south coast of Corsica, weaving traditional couscous-like rhythms with contemporary tapenade into a daube of power and diversity which exploits the full dynamic range of the absent clarinet.

The work will be performed in the atmospheric setting of the County Council Recycling Facility. Adm free. No cameras. Cushions.

ODIOUS MULTI SCREEN
Ring road, Grotton
Usual rubbish. See your local paper for details. Popcorn. Not recommended for people who actually want to watch films.

ARTS CINEMA
Snodgrass Centre Bletherley
Takamoto's award-winning 'Intellectual Pursuits of a Minor Government Official from the Kawasaki District', starring Sushi Quattro.

Sport and Leisure

COWPAT PARK STADIUM
Sweet FA Cup, 3rd round: Grotton Academicals reserves v Stockport County Juniors 4th team or Hyde Rangers (no need to book). KO 6.30 pm. Broadcast on Eurosport.

UNIVERSITY (PENDING) SPORTS CENTRE
Davidlock Road
Urban Extensions v New Settlements (amateur boxing match).

FREEMASONS HALL
Pioneer Street, Dunromin
Public Inquiry into proposed house extension. All seats bookable. St John's Ambulance in attendance. 20 August until 3 December (at least).

Where to eat

ROYAL GROTTON HOTEL
Station Approach, Sludge St
Traditional English service (allow three hours). High Tea in the Cunard Room. String trio. Round Table (Thurs).

VIEUX CHAPEAU
Authentic bistro atmosphere. Do not offend the manager.

BOGGART CLOUGH FOREST LODGE
Cloggley
Smørgasbørd øn draught. Tyrolean. Braces. Not recommended, but more reports please.

The following establishments can all be found on the Free Enterprise Industrial Trading Estate, Grotton Ring Road (on appeal in the late 1980s, in case you're wondering)
'Chips "n" Burgers'
'Burgers "n" Chips'
'Megaburgers "n" Fries'
'Southern Fried Curry "n" Chips'
'Chips "n" Pizza "n" Coke'
'Coke "n" Fries'
'Chicken, Coke, Chips, Pizza "n" burgers'

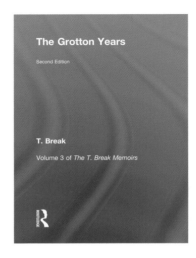

Invitation to the Secretary of State to speak at the Planning in Crisis Conference

Readers are advised that, as normal, the following exchange of e-mails should be read from the bottom up and not from the top down – in a sense not unlike the Government's planning polices.

From: Secretary.of.State@clg.gsi.gov.uk
To: Giles.Robbie-Williams@clg.gsi.gov.uk
Sent: Tuesday March 28th 2010 4.59 PM
Subject: Airports National Policy Statement

Oh bugger

JCB

From: Giles.Robbie-Williams@clg.gsi.gov.uk
To: Secretary.of.State@clg.gsi.gov.uk
Sent: Tuesday March 28th 2010 4.58 PM
Subject: Airports National Policy Statement

Secretary of State

As you will see, the News of the World are asking about your relationship with Mrs Harbringer-Grudge. Can you help with their queries?

Giles

From: Carolyn.Strange@dft.gsi.gov.uk
To: Giles.Robbie-Williams@clg.gsi.gov.uk
Sent: Tuesday March 28th 2010 4.57 PM
Subject: Airports National Policy Statement

Hi Giles

Unfortunately sent whole e-mail trail out with the press release!!!
Soz!!!! Easily done!!!

Can you help the News of the World?

Carrie

From: Kevin.Slyme@newsoftheworld.co.uk
To: Carolyn.Strange@dft.gsi.gov.uk
Sent: Tuesday March 28th 2010 4.56 PM
Subject: Airports National Policy Statement – interim statement

Yo Carrie

Thanks for e-mail. Tracked down Harbringer-Grudges but seem
to be away. Will get usual phone tap onto them but do you know
where they've gone? Police contact tells us there was an alleged
'incident' in 1992 which allegedly involved the S of S – any details
on that? Hope to have her medical records soon and there's a pap
outside the house so looks like a good 'un. Ta

Kev

Got a hot story? Tell us now! We pay £££

From: Carolyn.Strange@dft.gsi.gov.uk
To: Undisclosed recipients
Sent: Tuesday March 28th 2010 09.43 AM
Subject: Airports National Policy Statement – interim statement

/////////////////////// **PRESS RELEASE** ///////////////////////////

The forthcoming Airports National Policy Statement is a crucially important document, affecting as it does both our precious environment and the future of the economy (which of course is burgeoning under the stewardship of the present Government) directly. The Secretary of State for Transport wishes to ensure both that the environmental implications of this crucially important document and the views of stakeholders are taken fully into account. Unfortunately and entirely due to matters beyond the control of the Department, some of the necessary information about bats and some of the responses from our colleagues in the airlines industry are not yet to hand. The Policy Statement will therefore, exceptionally, be delayed for a short period. The Policy will of course be the better for this short delay and the Secretary of State anticipates being able to announce in due course an approach which will be acceptable to all, or at least some, interested parties.

C Strange (Ms)
Junior Press Liaison Auxiliary

From: <u>Giles.Robbie-Williams@clg.gsi.gov.uk</u>
To: <u>Carolyn.Strange@dft.gsi.gov.uk</u>
Sent: Friday March 24th 2010 10.16 AM

Hi Carrie

The S of S has given us a view on the airports policy – see below. I gather he's pretty insistent about it. Guess this means a further delay – no change there!!!!! Can you let this be known? Expect you can make it seem like a good thing!!!! Happy to chat anytime. Maybe a drink?

Cheers
Giles ☺

From: <u>Giles.Robbie-Williams@clg.gsi.gov.uk</u>
To: <u>Alexander.Quibble@gonw.gsi.gov.uk</u>
Sent: Friday March 24th 10.01 AM
Subject: Grotton Planning in Crisis Conference

Alexander

The Secretary of State has indicated his willingness to speak at your conference in September, unless of course some imperative exigency supervenes.

You will be aware of his usual requirements. He is a busy man and will arrive in a Government car at, or shortly after, the time he is due to speak. He will not take questions and he will leave briskly and immediately, but hopefully without causing offence. You should provide him with a good joke about the local area to use at the start of his speech, a glass of water with a little vodka, and adequate security to prevent the local press getting anywhere near him. He is unlikely to have time to meet the Harbringer-Grudges.

Please let me know if you have any further questions

Best
Giles

From: Secretary.of.State@clg.gsi.gov.uk
To: Giles.Robbie-Williams@clg.gsi.gov.uk
Sent: Thursday March 23rd 2010 8.22 PM
Subject: Grotton Planning in Crisis Conference

Giles

Yes OK as long as I can get out of it if Mrs JCB has other ideas. Will there be press coverage? Best avoid the Harbringer-Grudges.

JCB

PS I don't like the draft airports policy as it has specific proposals in it which affect places. This is always dangerous. Can it be watered down?

From: Giles.Robbie-Williams@clg.gsi.gov.uk
To: Secretary.of.State@clg.gsi.gov.uk
Sent: Friday March 10th 2010 5.41 AM
Subject: FW Grotton Planning in Crisis Conference

Secretary of State

I apologise if in my previous e-mail I implied anything other.

Would you like to speak at the conference?

Giles

PS While writing I wonder whether I could ask you yet again to let me have your views on the draft national policy statement on airports?

p 4 of 8

From: Secretary.of.State@clg.gsi.gov.uk
To: Giles.Robbie-Williams@clg.gsi.gov.uk
Sent: Friday March 10th 2010 5.34 PM
Subject: Grotton Planning in Crisis Conference

Giles

Though I have met Mrs Harbringer-Grudge in the past I can assure you
there is no more to it than that

JCB

From: Giles.Robbie-Williams@gsi.gov.uk
To: Secretary.of.State@clg.gsi.gov.uk
Sent: Wednesday March 1st 2010 8.05 AM
Subject: FW Grotton Planning in Crisis Conference

Secretary of State

I attach some details of Grotton from our North West brethren. The event
is of course during your holidays, and the place is difficult to get to, and
I understand rather dull when you arrive; but on the other hand Lieut-Col
Harbringer-Grudge of Cramshaw Superior has invited you to lunch (I am
told that Mrs Harbringer-Grudge is an old friend); and the main organiser
(Koffi Break) is from a BME group (you will recall you have targets to
meet people from those groups, which you are at present failing to meet).
So while the conference itself may be seen as being of little value you
might meet other political, social and equality objectives by agreeing to
attend. I am sure we will be able to recycle one of your speeches.

Your advice would be appreciated

Giles

From: Alexander.Quibble@gonw.gsi.gov.uk
To: Giles.Robbie-Williams@clg.gsi.gov.uk
Sent: Wednesday March 1st 2010 8.03 AM
Subject: Grotton Planning in Crisis Conference

Giles

I attach a short paper describing the location and history of Grotton.
I think you will find that the key fact, on page 127, is that it includes two
marginal constituencies.

I hope this will enable you to make a decision

Yours sincerely
Alexander

From: Giles.Robbie-Williams@clg.gsi.gov.uk
To: Alexander.Quibble@gonw.gsi.gov.uk
Sent: Tuesday February 29th 2010 10.23 PM
Subject: Grotton Planning in Crisis Conference

Alexander

The Secretary of State has asked me to ask you where Grotton is

Cheers
Giles

Diary Secretary to the Personal Private Secretary to the Secretary of State

---Original message----
From: Alexander.Quibble@gonw.gsi.gov.uk
To: Secretary.of.State@clg.gsi.gov.uk
Sent: Tuesday February 29th 2010 12.15 PM
Subject: Grotton Planning in Crisis Conference

Dear Secretary of State

Request to speak at Conference in Grotton

We have been asked whether you would be available to speak at an important conference entitled 'Planning in Crisis' in Grotton from 5–9 September. One of your predecessors, a Mr Heseltine, accepted an invitation to a previous conference under the same title in 1979. In fact he never turned up, and should you accept this invitation it would be a simple matter for us to find a plausible reason to follow the same course, as we have so often done in the past.

The conference is also to celebrate Grotton achieving 'average' status in this year's assessments; it is hard to under-state the significance of this, as you will appreciate if you know the history of the County.

We recommend that you accept the invitation to speak. We are able to remain entirely vague as to the content of your address until the last moment, and indeed we will be able to maintain that position for some time after the conference, should you find that helpful. You may have some important announcement to make (for example about the latest news on conservatory design in World Heritage Sites); or you may simply wish to follow the standard line and tell the planners to do everything faster with less resources.

Your humble and obedient servant
Alexander Quibble CB MA (Cantab) MBA
Regional Director, Government Office for the North West

An important appeal decision

Few students of planning law will remain unaware of the case of *Muckthorpe Estates (1998) plc v The First Secretary of State and Grimethwaite Borough Council.* In what was seen at the time as a landmark judgement (though still not without its critics), the Court of Appeal upheld the principle that fear of dreaming about being attacked by maggots could, in certain circumstances, be a material consideration, whether or not the maggots were housed in a purpose-built structure (Quelch, LJ, dissenting).

A study of the 2004 appeal decision which gave rise to the judicial review reveals in astonishing detail the range and complexity of the planning issues which modern-day Inspectors are required to deal with on a daily basis. Much, of course, has changed since then: for example, following the introduction by the Inspectorate of a 'least said, soonest mended' approach, decisions are now much shorter, being mostly scribbled on the back of a postcard. Nevertheless, the fundamental dilemmas facing the Planning Inspectorate in Bristol remain as challenging as ever.

The passage of time allows us to reflect on the robustness of Inspector Knaggs' original judgement in the case. Was he as clear in his reasoning on the conservation area point as he might have been? How well did he handle the materiality of the fourth consultation draft of the Local Plan First Review Issues Paper (to which he made no reference whatsoever)? And what do we think of the punctuation – should there really have been a comma after the word 'brown' in the fourth line of paragraph 5?

This historic appeal decision appears overleaf: readers are invited to judge for themselves.

The Planning Inspectorate

4/11 Budgerigar Wing
Temple Quay House
2 The Square
Temple Quay
Bristol BS1 6PN
☎ 0117 372 6372
"email":enquiries@pins.gsi.gov.uk

28 December 2004

DRAFT-NOT FOR ISSUE

Messrs Extend-u-Like
Architectural-type Services
4B Letsby Avenue
Just Behind the Launderette
GROTTON   GR9 8ZX

Your ref: LEM/£5,000/plusexpenses
Our ref: APP/GROT/A/05/409263
Ref are you blind:

Dear Sirs

TOWN AND COUNTRY PLANNING ACT 1990, SECTION 78 AND SCHEDULE 6
APPEAL BY MR LEMUEL PRESCOTT (NO RELATION)
APPLICATION REF: 00003/2004/FUL

1. As you know, I have been appointed by the "First Secretary of State" to determine this appeal against the failure of the Grimethwaite Borough Council to determine within the statutory period an application for planning permission for what is described on the application form as the erection of just a small shed really, on land to the rear of "Disraeli", 29 Rawalpindi Street, Grimethwaite. I have considered the written representations made by you and by the Council, and also those observations of the Grimethwaite Town Council which I was able to decipher. I visited the site on 23 December 2004.

2. The Council prefer to describe your client's proposal as "the erection of a 3-storey extension to existing maggot-breeding facility and ancillary worming compound, together with non-food retail warehouse and 200 space car park, following partial demolition of vacant listed synagogue", and I consider this to be a somewhat more accurate description of the appeal proposal.

3. On your client's behalf, you have suggested that since a synagogue falls within the same Use Class as a veterinary surgery, wherein sick animals are treated and cured, including on occasion, fish; and since the curing of fish and the breeding of maggots are themselves within the same Use Class; then it follows that no material change of use would be involved on the land. Most amusing.

4. You have also referred me to the case of Regina v Three Sewage Works Borough Council ex parte Mandelson, which you say you became aware of while inadvertently attending a Public Inquiry some years ago. You have, however, provided me with no further details of this case, and I regret to say that no-one here has ever heard of it. No matter.

5. At some point in time which you have been unable to recall, you submitted certain revisions to the original scheme in a commendable attempt to meet some of the Council's concerns. Drawing ref. Grot/04/Revision A shows the repositioning of three of the proposed mobile offal vats closer to the boundary with the adjacent Conservative club, and I intend to determine the appeal with that helpful amendment in mind. In addition, and following the site inspection, I received a brown, paper envelope, the contents of which I have referred to the appropriate authorities. Perhaps I could nevertheless take this opportunity of reciprocating your good wishes for Christmas and the New Year.

6. From my visit to the site and its surroundings, and from my reading of the written representations, I consider that the main issues in this case are:

(a).   the effect of the proposal on the character and appearance of the Grimethwaite Sidings Conservation Area; and

(b).   whether, so far as the retail element of the proposal is concerned, the requirements of the sequential test have been met.

7. I noted that, by the time of my visit, the former synagogue had been demolished. (That gives me one less thing to think about! No need to type that bit, dear).

8. The Statutory Development Plan for the area includes the Greater Grotton Structure Plan, but since the Council say that they have been unable to lay their hands on a copy of it since 1st April 1996, I am not in a position to accord its provisions much weight. You quote extensively from the Borough of Grimethwaite Development Plan, which was approved in 1951. However, the Council have asked me to have rather more regard to the provisions of the Grimethwaite Local Plan, adopted in 1997, on the principal grounds that, since they spent a considerable amount of time and effort in preparing it, it ought to be put to some use. I have my doubts, but we'll see how we get on.

9. Policy GEN1 describes the Council's broad approach to development in the Borough. In summary, this says that new development will generally be welcomed with open arms, so long as no-one can see any problems with it. You have pointed out that this policy has been the subject of objection from the Government Office of the North West, primarily on the grounds that only the Government is allowed to have policies like that. However, it seems to me that the Council's flexible and pragmatic approach to development control is based on sound planning principles, and I therefore propose to accord it considerable weight.

10. The Council also seem to be using an interim Supplementary Planning Guidance note on shopping, which says that developers will be required to locate new retail developments in town centres, except in those circumstances where they would really, really prefer not to. I understand that the wording of this policy, the status of which is somewhat obscure, is based on the draft of a speech delivered to a private meeting of the Multiple Shops Federation by a Mr Nicholas Ridley in 1987, and subsequently leaked to the Manchester Guardian. While no doubt a material consideration, it has been somewhat overtaken by events.

11. Turning then to the first issue, I noted from my visit that the character of the Grimethwaite Sidings Conservation Area derives principally from the close juxtaposition of an early Nineteenth Century waste-transfer station with two-storey terraced housing of little apparent merit. English Heritage have described the area as being a particularly good example of an early industrial slum, and who am I to disagree? The appeal site itself occupies a prominent position within the Conservation Area, being visible from those areas of the Kwiksave car-park where it appears safe to walk.

12. The plans as submitted indicated a building constructed primarily from corrugated iron sheeting and reclaimed asbestos panels. I have seen your client's response to the critical observations of the Society For The Preservation of the Few Decent Bits of Grimethwaite and note that he is now willing to face the main structure in Accrington brick, embellished as appropriate with Italian marble. However, para 17 of Planning Policy Guidance 1 points out that poor designs include those which are inappropriate to their context. I therefore consider the original submission to be preferable and have concluded that it would at least preserve the character and appearance of the conservation area.

13. So far as the second issue is concerned, I note what you say about the difficulties with the sequential test, but some poor bugger's got to try and sort it out, no, you'd better scrub that last bit, dear, and say "but the advice in Planning Policy Guidance 6 is clear."

14. I calculated that the appeal site lies approximately 296.4m from the eastern edge of the prime retail zone of Grimethwaite Town Centre, which the Council tentatively identify as the pie shop next to the Housing Benefits office. While this JUST allows the site to be categorised as "edge of centre" in the terms of PPG 6, I noted from my visit that it is separated from the rest of the town by a 40 foot high embankment carrying the 6-lane Grimethwaite Internal Relief Route. While national retail policy seeks to encourage linked trips, I consider it unlikely that many town centre shoppers will attempt to negotiate this obstacle, especially while carrying a bucket of maggots.

15. The Council have produced a schedule of 14 town centre sites which they say are suitable and available for the retail element of your client's operation, and which therefore would accord with national and local policy. I consider that little weight can be attached to this evidence, however, since none of them are actually within Grimethwaite. (I record here the Council's explanation that this evidence was submitted as a result of "an administrative error" but, being a civil servant, that is not a term with which I am familiar).

16. I have concluded that the requirements of the sequential test would, or quite possibly would not, be met by the appeal proposal.

17. The Council have also made reference to what they describe as "an appalling stench" associated with the existing operation; and they have pointed out that, despite there being no specific policy, it has become their practice to require new industrial development to be acceptable in terms of its impact on any adjacent residential accommodation. You have accepted that, during the maggot-fattening phase of the production cycle, residents of the Lakelands Estate at Muckthorpe Bottoms are obliged to close all doors and windows for at least 2 days. You do not, however, concede that this results in any conflict with policy, since you say that the estate is not adjacent to the appeal site, being over 5 miles away to the north. While I have a somewhat uneasy feeling about the robustness of any conclusions to be drawn from this analysis, I have insufficient evidence on the matter to arrive at a firm conclusion as to its merit.

17a. I have taken into account the separate but related concerns of Mrs Prototype of 17 Windermere View, whose home overlooks the site, and whose husband suffers from a rare medical condition which causes him to fear dreaming of being sexually abused by large maggots. As far as I am able to discern, the *Journal of Planning and Environmental Law* contains only

2

one reference to the materiality of fear of maggots (of whatever size or habit) to decisions on planning applications, and in that case (unlike the appeal proposal) the maggots were free to roam at will. I am therefore not persuaded, on balance, and on the basis of the available evidence, that this is a matter to which significant weight need necessarily be accorded, generally speaking (although, for the avoidance of doubt, I really have thought about it).

18. Turning now to other matters, I fully accept that paragraph 12.8 of Regional Planning Guidance Note 13 is material to my consideration of the case. I do not, however, share your views that maggot-breeding, even in the context of Grimethwaite, could reasonably be described as "a sunrise industry". While I do not doubt your assertion that, should the appeal fail, your client would have to lay off Mrs Braithwaite, from what she has told me, that's not a moment too soon. As to other more general concerns, I have some sympathy with the fact that the wife's mother has been unwell; and I am the first to recognise that hernias are both painful and embarrassing. However, neither this nor any of the other considerations is sufficient to outweigh the risk to highway safety which would flow from the proposal, and which I probably should have mentioned earlier.

20. Finally, I have noted that your client has elected not to sign a S106 Agreement which, if permission were to be granted, would require him to carry out certain works before the building is occupied, and I consider that he is justified in describing the Council's demands as being contrary to the spirit of national guidance. In particular, this applies to the construction of a new transport interchange, a community forest, and an extension to the bar in the Members' Lounge.

21. I have considered all the other matters raised in the representations, including your reference to Planning Policy Guidance 20 on Coastal Planning and the Council's observation that Grimethwaite lies some 35 miles east of the Irish Sea at Southport. However, nothing I have read makes the slightest difference to my conclusions.

22. For the reasons set out above, and in exercise of the powers transferred to me, I hereby dismiss this pointless appeal.

23. I am, Sirs, your obedient servant,

Arnold Knaggs **BSc MIMunE FRTPI**

an Inspector appointed by the then Minister of Housing and Local Government

Right, that's it dear, what's for dinner?

The Dunromin Design Guide

Dunromin has long longed to have its own design guide. Everything from handy hints for anyone designing an airport runway down to a chapter called 'Dos and Don'ts for Decent Doors' is covered in the 350-page document, which has now been handsomely produced on recycled Environmental Impact Assessments just in time for the Planning in Crisis Conference.

It is the ground-breaking chapter on 'Garden Gnomes' which has been the subject of such attention at national level. This is a difficult and emotive subject, and previous guides have shied away from it. Gnomes (and the planners have shrewdly drawn the definition widely enough to include pixies, elves and frogs) have become increasingly popular in the County but, as the Guide says, 'the boom period of the 1990s resulted in a rash of speculative gnomes, generally badly designed and poorly constructed, and some action was obviously needed'.

'Careful consideration of the relevant design constraints,' says the Guide, pointedly, 'will help in the production of a harmonious and spatially balanced resolution of the competing elements, and the ultimate reconciliation of form and function.'

Advice in the Guide doesn't always sit easily with the aspirations of local home owners, as the following examples show:

HEIGHT
Maximum gnome height will normally be three metres, and it should be necessary to exceed this only in very special circumstances. As far as possible the gnome should not be the dominant feature in the landscape – in many ways the impact can be greater if it remains subordinate to the surrounding buildings. It would normally be inappropriate for the girth to exceed twice the height.

MATERIALS
Concrete gnomes weather badly and should be avoided. The toadstool should be of a design which is in sympathy with the shape and markings of local species. (Toadstools indigenous to Dunromin do *not* have spots.)

FACIAL EXPRESSION
A successful scheme will reflect the character of the locality. Restraint is essential in Conservation Areas, where a sober and dignified demeanour will minimise visual dislocation. Parts of the area will, however, benefit from the careful positioning of gnomes of a more jocular disposition.

DIVERSITY
Suitable arrangements should be made for gnomes with disabilities. Gnomes are almost exclusively of the male gender; the inclusion of female gnomes would be political correctness gone mad.

THE TOADSTOOL ENVELOPE
As a minimum requirement toadstools should be designed to Level 6 (zero carbon) standards as set out in the 'Code for Sustainable Gnomes'. Gnomes engaged in fishing should utilise sustainably managed stocks.

The Guide does not of course deal with matters such as the need for gnomes to be located close to public transport routes, density and parking standards, or affordable gnomes; these, naturally, are matters for the LDF. Environmental Elf has been involved as both noise and air pollution are affecting gnomic lifestyles.

Some of the principles developed to deal with gnomes clearly have a resonance in other areas. For example the Commission for Architecture and the Built Environment (CABE) commend the following advice on housing:

CONFUSION OF SCALE LEADS TO UNSATISFACTORY COMPOSITION OF FORM.

INCONGRUITY OF SCALE

USE OF VISUALLY WEAK ROOF SUPPORT GIVES UNSTABLE APPEARANCE

LACK OF VISUAL STRENGTH

TWO HANDLES PRODUCE DUALITY OF FORM – CONFUSING TO THE EYE

*NOTE GNOME AND TOADSTOOL FOR SCALE REFERENCE

UNRESOLVED DUALITY

DOWNRIGHT INCOMPETENCE

Every site is bound to have its advantages and disadvantages. In Dunromin's case of course the former tend to predominate. This does not mean that the *genius loci* is any less important though it is always tempting to ignore it in the hope that it will go away.

Architects and designers should recognise that buildings on sloping sites have a tendency to fall over unless special care is taken.

The division of the dwelling house into a number of rooms, while having certain functional advantages, usually increases costs and reduces the all-important element of flexibility. From our original research, it seems that the larger rooms become the more space they contain. Designers should take advantage of this principle by making some rooms bigger than others.

The problem of residential extensions, and the increasing incomprehensibility of the General Permitted Development Order, can best be addressed by building the extension at the same time as the original house.

The RTPI has shortlisted the Guide for an award. Judges were particularly impressed that a chapter on housing had been written without a mention of BedZed. The Dunromin Design Guide is clearly essential reading for every architect and developer in the region, and should be of equal interest to the average person in the communal pedestrian circulatory interspace. It is in fact a powerful reminder of just how useful a planning department can be if it isn't very careful. Perhaps its importance is best summed up by Barbara Turpentine herself in an extract from the introduction to the guide:

'I must stress that this is only a guide. It is not for us to tell you architects how to do your job. That's a matter for the Prince of Wales. So if you want to go ahead and ignore the whole thing, that's fine. But I should warn you that if you do decide that's what you'd rather do, I may be unable to restrain my planning committee from adopting the kind of unhelpful attitude for which they are admired throughout the Royal Borough.'

Appeal by Alexander Quibble CB
GOVERNMENT OFFICE FOR THE REGION

I am grateful for the opportunity provided by the authors of this great book to make this appeal on behalf of the Ebenezer Howard Home for Distressed Planners. It's a sort of planning appeal really.

The home is in Swindon, where recovering patients can be taken to see the finest examples of the town planner's art. Tours of the North East township, taking in a medium sized branch of Halfords, and ending at the coffee bar on the mezzanine floor of Sainsbury's, which sadly does not have the benefit of planning permission, are of course legendary.

There are many individuals caught up in planning who simply find themselves unable to cope. The purpose of the home is to provide shelter from the everyday stresses of the modern high-speed world of local authority planning. It has seen many sad case histories, but none more disturbing than that of Arthur Smallpiece – or 'Eight-weeks Arthur', as he likes to be known. He prefers to remain anonymous, but his name is indeed Arthur Smallpiece, and he lives at 43 Proposed Inner Distributor Road, Grotton GR1 1DC.

Arthur is addicted to development control. He was first attracted to it, like so many others, by the romance, the adventure, the danger, the beautiful women. At first all was well. He used to operate the office coffee machine, and moved on to putting fresh paper in the printer.

But problems soon began. He started to enter applications in the register as soon as they arrived – even though he knew the office policy was to send them all back and ask for further information. He moved on to sniffing development plans, and would slip away to the lavatory to read the General Permitted Development Order (as amended).

Then, one day, he took an application home with him. It was only a householder one. He didn't mean it any harm. He just wanted to be near it. But soon it was two or three every night, then whole armfuls. His colleagues made things worse

Arthur Smallpiece, who wishes to remain anonymous
(photo courtesy of National Museum of Applied Bureaucracy, Eland House, London)

by helping him to carry them to the lift and advising him not to bother bringing them back.

Inevitably, the time came when he decided to determine an application himself. It would be the ultimate experience. He stayed late one night. There was nobody about. He allowed his fingers to hover for a few delicious moments over the keyboard, savouring the experience, and before he could stop himself he had allowed a change of use from a chip shop to an old folks' home. With – and this was particularly exciting – several conditions.

He exploded with joy and relief. It was a feeling like the feeling he imagined you would get when you lost your virginity except that he didn't know what that felt like because he hadn't.

It was a slippery slope, of course. Things went from bad to worse. His colleagues did what they could for him. Naturally they tried promoting him, but it was too late. They tried aversion therapy – they sent him to meetings with engineers, and even seconded him to English Heritage, where they thought he might be weaned off the idea that actually making decisions was important.

But none of this worked and soon it began to affect his family life. He used to get his wife to dress up as an Environmental Impact Assessment, then give her a ruling – on a case-by-case basis – as to whether she exceeded the indicative thresholds and criteria set out in the table in Schedule 2 of the Regulations. Eventually she ran off with someone from the County Planning Department who convinced her that a 'Structure Plan' was a form of homoeopathic treatment with effects similar to those of Viagra.

For Arthur that was the end of the world. And that's where Swindon comes in. I am sure you can find it in your hearts to feel compassion for people like him – sensitive, vulnerable and above all victims of an oppressive and uncaring system. Help us to help them. If you have any unwanted planning applications lying around, a hatstand, some red tape, that you don't know what to do with, send them to me, A Quibble, at the Government Office. I will put them to good use.[1] It means so little to you, but so much to the poor souls incarcerated in Swindon.

Please give generously.

Thank you.

1 If you prefer to send cash, it is probably
   safer to send it to the authors.

Index